The Unidentified Modern City
Globalized Brescia

What is an "Unidentified Modern City"? Like a UFO, it is something we imagine our present or future to be, something we live in, but would expect to be completely different from how we had planned it. Are today's modern cities the result of the failure of a modernist utopia or are they merely the product of a process of adapting ideas regarding our future life, as applied to urban development tailored to suit contemporary lifestyles?

This question is what triggered the idea of the exhibition, in which Gabriele Basilico, one of the most important contemporary architectural photographers, encounters Dan Graham, one of the great Conceptual artists, who has thoroughly investigated the relationship between public and private in cities today. The surprising result of this survey and this encounter is that modern architecture, with its lack of identity, is only meaningful if viewed through the eyes of the people who live in it.

What links these two artists is the discovery of a new social class that reflects its behavior and identity in architecture. Surprisingly, while town planners consider the "Unidentified Modern City" as representing the unsuccessful result of a modernist utopia, the two artists focus on an urban space that points to a new social lifestyle and the birth of a new collective entity, in short, the establishment of a new, positive standard of living within a building that has lost its original significance.

A close look at Basilico's and Graham's pictures clearly shows us that their apparent focus on architecture—often without the presence of inhabitants—conceals a great interest in the social relations that this type of architecture has redefined, those that involve us in the "Unidentified Modern City."

The subject of this survey is Brescia, a medium-sized town in north Italy. The two artists have analyzed aspects Brescia has in common with numerous towns in other countries with the same architectural characteristics, regardless of the size: Lyon or Nice in France, Manchester or Liverpool in England, Frankfurt in Germany, San Francisco in the United States, and Gwangju in Korea. The artists' work intersects to produce a dialogue, a reflection on the urban space of a town portrayed in its more recent development, revealing in its apparent anomie the identity of a middle class common to many towns elsewhere in the world. The two viewpoints of the artists offer perspectives that overlap to produce a third point of view.

Gabriele Basilico appears to observe the town, creating relations between a building and the rest of the urban setting to which it belongs. Dan Graham focuses more on details, parts of the town, as if his observation identified with the state of flux of those accustomed to living in it. The Omnia Struttura building photographed by Graham is an emblematic representation of modular, commonplace architecture that is infinitely replicated in modern towns, in the East and West, in Europe, the United States, and Asia alike. But this possibility of repetition contains the seed of a new lifestyle identity. The repetitiveness of the architecture holds a new identity—or absence of it—that represents a new community style, which is a gesture of liberation from all predefined social identity. It is the affirmation of a social status that is outside the possibilities of a life designed at the drawing board.

We find these same features in other shots by Dan Graham, as in the loggia with the shop bearing the "Intermedia" logo, in the shelter for the supermarket trolleys, in the long shoe-shop window with the large poster of the smiling teenager. Her face appears to belong to one of the inhabitants of this new urban area. The window reflects the surrounding architectural structures, the effect being very similar to that of the semi-reflective glass the artist uses for his pavilions. In this picture, the girl's face blends with the reflected urban environment, and the result is a perfect representation of urban space within the "Unidentified Modern City."

Basilico turns his attention more to individual buildings or parts of them, which are photographed with absolute objectivity and precision. In their apparent isolation, these buildings relate continually to the surrounding urban fabric, and despite the absence of their inhabitants, make continuous reference to them. The photograph of the Tintoretto Tower in the San Polo district—with satellite dishes at the windows, washing hung out to dry, and air-conditioning units dotting the colored stripes marking the storeys—becomes a representation of the people who live there, though no one appears in the picture.

Like those in San Polo, the buildings in Brescia 2 are photographed at times from afar, and are almost always linked to a road that often occupies most of the picture. In Basilico's photographs, the road is just as important as the building, since it acts as a link and enables the town to be lived in. Roads are a tangible representation of the fact that the buildings he photographs are places in which social relations are established.

The point of encounter of the two artists involved in this project is the positive interpretation they both give of the contemporary town, which links Brescia to many of the world's other cities. They both explore the concept defined today as "globalization," which has remodeled the very concept of urban conglomeration. For Dan Graham, the interior of a McDonald's near the eastern ring road represents a setting revealing a new humanity that survives happily within the town, with no memories of the past. One of Graham's most significant images is that of a window of purple clothes, with the price tags clearly visible. In its objectivity, the picture describes the people who dwell in these urban areas, the new, apparently anonymous and traditionless middle class that represents the identity of everyone within the contemporary city.

Both artists describe the aspects of the town that make it less identifiable, yet viable at the same time. Architecture within which are formed, and which models relationships between people. The buildings featuring dream-like modernism identified by Basilico are the new possibilities offered by the contemporary town, even when the architecture appears to be contradictory and to have failed to implement its utopian vision. Basilico's keenly objective eye captures, in some parts of Brescia 2, a Martian depiction of architecture, in which people find themselves living in a present that is more like an improbable future. The buildings he photographs are seen as naked objects, representing not an ideology, that of the modern city, but rather the plain construction in relation to the body of the town. There is no halo of modernity in these images, just what the inhabitants see there. Basilico's vision as an architect dedicated to photography is that of someone who has managed to shrug off all preconceptions, and view architecture democratically, as do the inhabitants. His photograph of the new headquarters of Banco di Brescia is a sunny, positive, and optimistic image.

Basilico's work reveals a democratic approach that he shares with Dan Graham. The American artist emphasizes the details that represent the flux of a town and its inhabitants, as can be seen in his pictures of shop windows. The roof over the supermarket trolleys provides a place of shelter, or rest for items used by people in their daily lives, drawing inspiration from the architecture or even inspiring it. The purpose behind all Dan Graham's work on the town is to display relationships created by architecture. Gabriele Basilico's objectivity and Dan Graham's apparently casual representations, which converge in this exhibition, come together in a dual vision, one intent on capturing the true nature of the place surveyed, the other on showing us the urban area as an interstitial place where human relations are redefined. This dual approach produces a new view of architecture in the contemporary urban space of an "Unidentified Modern City." The contemporary town in this case is Brescia, with its stretches of ordinary buildings, which the two artists reinterpret from the perspective of those who live there. What emerges from this field research is the democratization that arises from this type of unidentified architecture, which Gabriele Basilico and Dan Graham, in their own different ways, know how to highlight.

—Maurizio Bortolotti

A Dialogue

Could architecture be the subject that allows an exchange betwen us, and an interaction?

Gabriele Basilico & Dan Graham

GB Dear Dan, first of all I would like to thank you for accepting Minini Gallery's invitation to join me in setting up an exhibition in Brescia curated by Maurizio Bortolotti. They have asked us to conduct a written dialogue to bear witness to our work in Brescia, which will be published in a book.

The first question does not come easily. You are universally recognized in the world of art as an artist who has worked conceptually on various topics, with projects linked to intersubjectivity and relationships with space and places, using diverse languages ranging from video to performance to installation.

I photograph buildings and urban landscapes and for over 30 years I have been obsessed with recording the things I want to capture. At times I feel rather like a collector of pictures of towns who wants to complete his series but never manages to stop taking photographs… Could architecture be the subject that allows an exchange between us, and an interaction?

I, with my obsessively repetitive method, you, with your speculative and philosophical approach and the development of a theoretical way of thinking that continues to renew itself.

A person who has played a key role in terms of the quality of his work and its ethical dimension becomes a necessary reference at this point in the subject, which can occupy the entire life of an artist or a man. I am talking about Walker Evans, with his extraordinary ability to discover and recount people and places in a rigorously aesthetic and highly respectful way. I would call him a man with a vision that is straightforward, fair, and refined at the same time.

There was an exhibition in Rotterdam in 1992 that showed your work in relation to that of Walker Evans. I have never seen the catalogue unfortunately, so I am not in a position to make any comments. But I do want to ask you simply and directly: What effect did Evans' personality have on you, and how do you relate to it in your work as an artist and researcher?

DG You ask me about my relation to Walker Evans.

Although I am not directly influenced by his work, I feel an affinity in that his work makes use of the magazine page and is in the genre of photojournalism. We both relate to seriality as in Minimal art and billboard

> We both relate to seriality as in Minimal art and billboard images as in Pop art. I think we were both fascinated by the petit bourgeois on the edge of the industrial rural slums. In other words, the edge of the city's urbanism.

images as in Pop art. I think we were both fascinated by the petit bourgeois on the edge of industrial rural slums. In other words, the edge of the city's urbanism.

Your work seems to be involved with the postwar Italian city in terms of the new urban plan. Have you been influenced by Aldo Rossi's book The Architecture of the City?

GB Aldo Rossi was a person of great importance to me, as he was for architectural culture as a whole and for the debate that arose in Italy and elsewhere in Europe after 1968. I met him in the 1960s when he was teaching at the Milan Polytechnic's Faculty of Architecture where I was a student.

His book The Architecture of the City (1966) was—and still is—a fundamental text around which the architectural debate revolves. Rossi's analytical method of comparing single buildings with the urban fabric, of giving depth to history in dialoguing with the modern, his respect and study of the locus are some of the strengths of his untiring research.

The notion of "urban fact," the theme of the relationship with the history of the city and monuments (theory of permanence), and insistent analysis of types are but some of the topics that have related architecture to philosophy and art, and have animated scholars and schools of architecture for decades.

As regards the identity of place, the main theme of photographic research in the 1970s, Aldo Rossi wrote: "Every place is undoubtedly singular to the extent to which it possesses endless affinities or analogies with other places. Even the concept of identity, and hence foreign-ness, is relative." "I've always claimed that places are stronger than people, fixed scenes are stronger than happenings." "In my opinion place and time are the first condition of architecture, so the hardest [...] After the 1980s, photography in Italy and the rest of Europe, committed to observing the new urban landscape, was influenced by American art and the theoretical debate that marked the previous decades. I remember Robert Venturi's books Complexity and Contradiction in Architecture (1966) and Learning from Las Vegas (1972), important volumes in the open discussions of the postmodern era, not only for architecture, but for the art world in general."

I have a question for you now: How has Robert Venturi's way of thinking influenced your life?

DG Robert Venturi's way of thinking was very important to me. He truly loves the same art I loved—Ed Ruscha and Claes Oldenburg. His understanding of upper-lower-class suburban vernacular architecture was extremely important to me. I think that there is a real relation Aldo Rossi's use of poetic vernacular and Venturi's use of poetry and wit in his work. My favorite Venturi is his museum for Benjamin Franklin for the American Biennial in Philadelphia. I've met Venturi and he's a very sweet person. In an interview I did with him he mentioned that he would like to retire to Northern New Jersey—the Italian upper-middle-class suburbs that also influenced me. It interests him to see the neighboring New York skyline from New Jersey. (His wife Denise Scott Brown says, "This is a nightmare I hope will never happen.")

> **The inventory of shapes that Aldo Rossi rediscovered and relaunched as a fragment for a recomposition of the city—a "Rossian collage city," as Colin Rowe calls it—doesn't appear to contain an ironic allusion, rather it is rooted in history, in the search for a geometric rigor and essentiality of architecture.**

GB Dear Dan, I have never been lucky enough to meet Robert Venturi, but his two books Complexity and Contradiction and Learning from Las Vegas caused a great deal of comment in Europe. They can be said to have caused a revolution in thinking, in the criticism of modernism, making a clean sweep of that reverential fear that was the ideological credo of so many generations after Bauhaus.

Venturi has taught us to look at the world around us with new, disenchanted eyes, to observe and accept the landscape and the town with curiosity, with attention—I would almost say democratically—finally putting on the same plane refined architecture, that by the great designers, and ordinary, commonplace architecture, where the ephemeral, superstructural language of advertising has been integrated with or replaced building construction, concealing it.

This visual and critical approach, which we can ultimately define as "democratic"—without or without rhetoric—has been fundamental for architecture and for art. Even photography has embraced it fully, as in the case of Ed Ruscha's fascinating research in his Twenty-six Gasoline Stations (1963).

I have been working on towns and urban landscapes for 30 years or so. It all started in 1978 with a project on the industrial suburbs of Milan, the town I was born and still live in. At that time there were already many abandoned areas next to factories still in operation. I was really fascinated by Bernd & Hilla Becher's Anonyme Skulpture, the frontal rigor with which they photographed various types of industrial archaeology in black and white, their cataloguing, their taxonomic approach to the project, their maniacal, obsessive, and potentially infinite research.

My work on the outskirts of my town, which led a few years later to an exhibition and a book entitled Milano Ritratti di Fabbriche (1978–1980), never had the rigor or purity of the Bechers' work, nor the equidistant viewpoint of Ed Ruscha's. It is a work on spaces, streets, and places, and is undoubtedly influenced by the photographic style, which, from the 1930s onward, with the Farm Security Administration's mission, had unequivocally conditioned the world of documentary photography. I refer again here to the teachings of the great Walker Evans, with his comprehensive and rigorous approach, aesthetic yet uncondescending, and to his definition/notion of "documentary style." Walker Evans' pictures are the expression

I see a parallel between Rossi and Venturi's work in that both deal with childhood memories of the vernacular suburban architectural landscape in a poetic (and in Rossi's case, cinematic, phantasmagoric) manner.

of an ethical vision; in the words of my friend Luigi Ghirri, they are "like caressing the world."

Talking about these approaches and the influence of these important protagonists of culture and artistic research, it is evident that the field, the object of analyses and ideas, is still the town itself.

Seen the other way round, the town itself provides an opportunity for comparing only apparently diverging theories and thoughts, like those of Robert Venturi and Aldo Rossi.

It has already been noted that in the recovery of the vernacular town, discounting the obvious difference between Europe and America, Robert Venturi's critical approach implies an ironic attitude, which is vital for a thorough, unprejudiced understanding of the identity of the new urban landscape.

The inventory of shapes that Aldo Rossi rediscovered and relaunched as a fragment for a recomposition of the city—a "Rossian Collage City," as Colin Rowe calls it—does not appear to contain an ironic allusion, rather it is rooted in history, in the search for geometric rigor and essentiality of architecture.

When I saw your photographs of Brescia, especially the objects you captured—shop windows, road signs, parked cars, doors, windows, fences, barriers, fragments of a chaotic and confused urban landscape—my thoughts inevitably went back to other pictures and to other photographers and artists. For example, the street pictures by Lee Friedlander came to mind, but they are obviously more constructed, more thoroughly "photographic," whereas yours are more like true documents, apparently less dependent on the construction of a style. Would you agree? And what do you have to say about this?

DG Venturi's work didn't directly influence my early photographs of New Jersey suburban houses, roadside factories, and signage, but after discovering his architectural work, such as the Guild House and the Lieb House on the New Jersey coast, two of my first architectural models, *Alteration of a Suburban House* and *Video Projection Outside Home* (1978) were in response to his work. Venturi's Lieb House period work noted the symbolism of the typical ornamental decoration outside Italian-American owned single-family houses, such as a plastic Madonna in the birdbath placed next door to the Lieb House.

My placement of a large video projector on the front lawn of a house displaying whatever was on the family's inside TV set was intended to create an emblem of the family's lifestyle on the roadside for passing observers. It relates to the proposed "gold"-painted TV antenna on top of the Guild House for retired Quaker families in Philadelphia, the intention of which was to symbolize the custom of retired residents watching television while resting in their rooms.

Venturi was directly influenced by Ed Ruscha's photographs, as well as by Pop artists such as Claes Oldenburg. I see a parallel between Rossi and Venturi's work in that both deal with childhood memories of the vernacular suburban architectural landscape in a poetic (and in Rossi's case, cinematic, phantasmagoric) manner. Rossi's Modena Cemetery reminds me of the interior of a suburban shopping mall. Venturi's use of irony is more about wit than about being caustic or critical. Finally, both architects are drawn to seaside houses or makeshift seaside shelters.

THE ARCHITECT'S NEWSPAPER MARCH 7, 2007

DIALOGUE:

ROBERT VENTURI, DENISE SCOTT BROWN, AND DAN GRAHAM

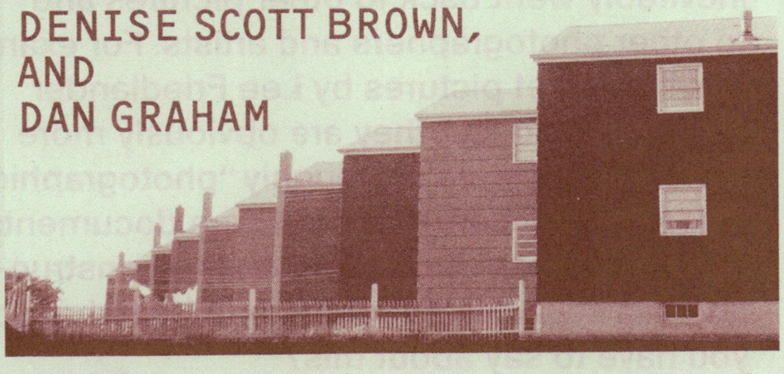

The artist Dan Graham's work has long been influenced by architecture, and his photographs of New Jersey capture an essential beauty of that state's vernacular landscape. (*Dan Graham's New Jersey* is up at Columbia University's Arthur Ross Architecture Gallery through March 23.) His love of both high and low architecture is shared by Robert Venturi and Denise Scott Brown, and Graham has written about the couple's American Pop Art approach in his essay "The City as Museum." *The Architect's Newspaper* went along to listen in on a conversation between the three in the offices of Venturi, Scott Brown and Associates in Manayunk, Pennsylvania.

Dan Graham: I want to talk about humor: I think your work is very funny, poetic, and humorous at the same time.

Denise Scott Brown: Architecture tends toward the monumental because of its size, and we use humor to tone that down. If you are a little self-deprecating, you take the wind out of your monumental sails.

Eero Saarinen also had a tremendous sense of humor, and you worked with him.

Robert Venturi: I don't see humor in his work.

I'm talking about the dormitory Hill College House (1960) at the University of Pennsylvania.

DSB: People say the alternating vertical and horizontal windows across the faces are like girls that nod and shake their heads. But I don't think that came from Saarinen. [When it opened, Hill College House was a women's dormitory.]

RV: I think the humor comes from other people. Saarinen merely meant his work to be an architectural expression; I've never been sympathetic to

...

but it was because they changed the way the building was used. Change is understandable, but you should try to ask, "What was the intention here?"

RV: This is a problem with institutional buildings, which last a long while. When you design according to the needs of the original users, later administrators may change the program.

I once wrote an article on your architecture and mentioned Aldo Rossi for contrast, but now I think Rossi is also a vernacular architect.

RV: Yes, but I think he had a more literal connection with history than we did. Rossi's vernacular is Italian, and because Italian architecture has been a source for American architects, we interpret the Italian vernacular as historical—it's part of our history.

But since your work is American, it is immediate and present with historic echoes. This is the American way. Have you had any chance to see any new Japanese architecture? I love the work of Itsuko Hasagawa, for example.

RV: I do not keep up with current architecture because it generally does not interest me. I keep up with everyday architecture. But we have written about how we love the architecture of Japan and how much we have learned from and been inspired by it. We traveled there in the 1990s, but no longer have work there. I loved three things in Japan: the everyday of now—like the great eclectic mess of signage on the Ginza—and the historical architecture and gardens of Kyoto. Thirdly, I love the Buddhist architecture of Nikko. We still celebrate the first day we went to Japan as we celebrate the first day I went to Rome.

DSB: We knew about Japanese historical and modern architecture before we went there, but when we arrived, we discovered the urbanism from the 1950s and 1960s. It is exuberant, impolite, funny, and wonderful, and has a kind of naïve, semimodernist influence from American magazines, but done much better.

There are always signs is English!

RV: I love the signs!

Massimo Minini, Dan Graham, Gabriele Basilico.

MM Brescia is a town like many others elsewhere in the world. And, like many other towns in Italy, it has a beautiful historic center with important ancient monuments, besides being one of the country's leading industrial centers. I asked two artists—a photographer and a non-photographer—to take pictures of the town for me. The result was two very different portrayals of Brescia: Gabriele Basilico tackled the job from a professional point of view, Dan Graham viewed it more remotely, like an American tourist. So we have two opposing attitudes and highly different outcomes. Why did both of you concentrate more on the suburbs rather than the old town center? And why did Dan focus mostly on details?

DG Dear Massimo, the focus of my photographs on the postwar suburban edge of Brescia was definitely influenced by my childhood experience of growing up on the suburban edge of New York City. The landscape of my childhood was shopping malls, proto-McDonald's fast-food restaurants, low-density manufacturing, and small office "shed"

Brescia is a town like many others elsewhere in the world. And, like many other towns in Italy, it has a beautiful historic center with important ancient monuments, besides being one of the country's leading industrial centers.

buildings. These were all located on the new highway low-density expansion in the suburbs. I have photographed both the New Jersey and Brescia houses of working class families who have, in their new housing facades, moved to the petit bourgeois (lower middle class), represented in the faux "neo classicist" street facades with connotations of faux luxury in their decorative details.

GB What interests me most when I look at a town is its recent physical transformation. I like to see how the urban fabric has evolved, and this has been happening up until yesterday, often in the areas around the city, on the outskirts. I too am aware of the great architectural works, both historic and contemporary, but I think the town is all this together, architecture and ordinary buildings, the co-existence of different places that often become disorder and anarchy, precisely where a photographer can look closely and try to create harmony and balance out of chaos.

Alvaro Siza, who wrote the preface to my book Cityscapes (1999), describes how you can look at an urban phenomenon from different viewpoints. "Twenty or so years ago, Carlos Nelson, a Brazilian architect, arrived in Portugal. He was in charge of the reconstruction of a favela in Rio de Janeiro. He presented his project by projecting slides showing the work in progress. A colorful blend of urban struggle, 'self-construction,' samba, and poetry. He wanted to write a book, and had already thought of the title: 'From the Favela to the City.' I was moved by the idea of a renewed city—what sort, I don't know—that would rise from the suburbs, from the bidonvilles, from the favelas more than from the memory of historic town centers."

In Brescia I picked the area to the south of the town, the other side of the motorway and railway. The part that has developed like a new town, a tertiary city that can hold a few mini-skyscrapers, a few blocks of flats and rows of terraced houses, a long green rectangle (possibly a future town park?) featuring an architectural style somewhere between postmodernism and neomodernism. I enjoyed combining the pictures recounting this very recent urban expansion with other photographs dedicated to a social housing estate built to the southeast of Brescia in the 1970s. A series of parallel terraced houses form a system, linked by raised walkways, with unlikely town gates marking the accesses to vast rows of houses. Not to mention the tall, compact buildings, streamlined and colorful, perforated by hundreds of windows, that rise perpendicular to the web of horizontal rows, like landmarks that can be seen from a long way off. A few photographs were dedicated to the Piazza della Vittoria, where both a disembowelment and monumental reconstruction that took place right in the center; they bear witness to the first urban intervention in modern times, completed during the era of the Fascist regime.

> **The landscape of my childhood was shopping malls, proto-McDonald's fast-food restaurants, low-density manufacturing, and small office "shed" buildings.**

I think the town is all this together, architecture and ordinary buildings, the co-existence of different places that often become disorder and anarchy, precisely where a photographer can look closely and try to create harmony and balance out of chaos.

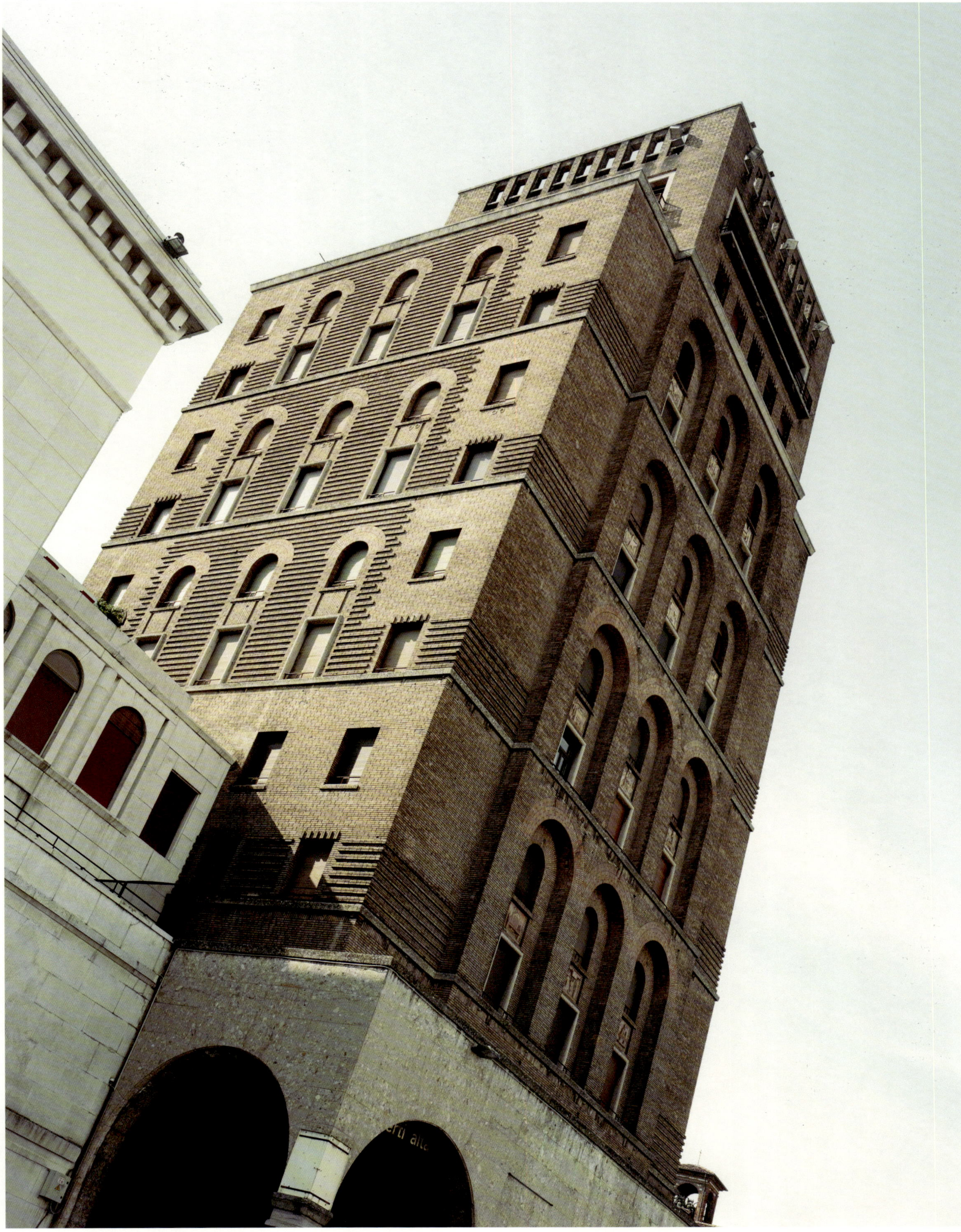

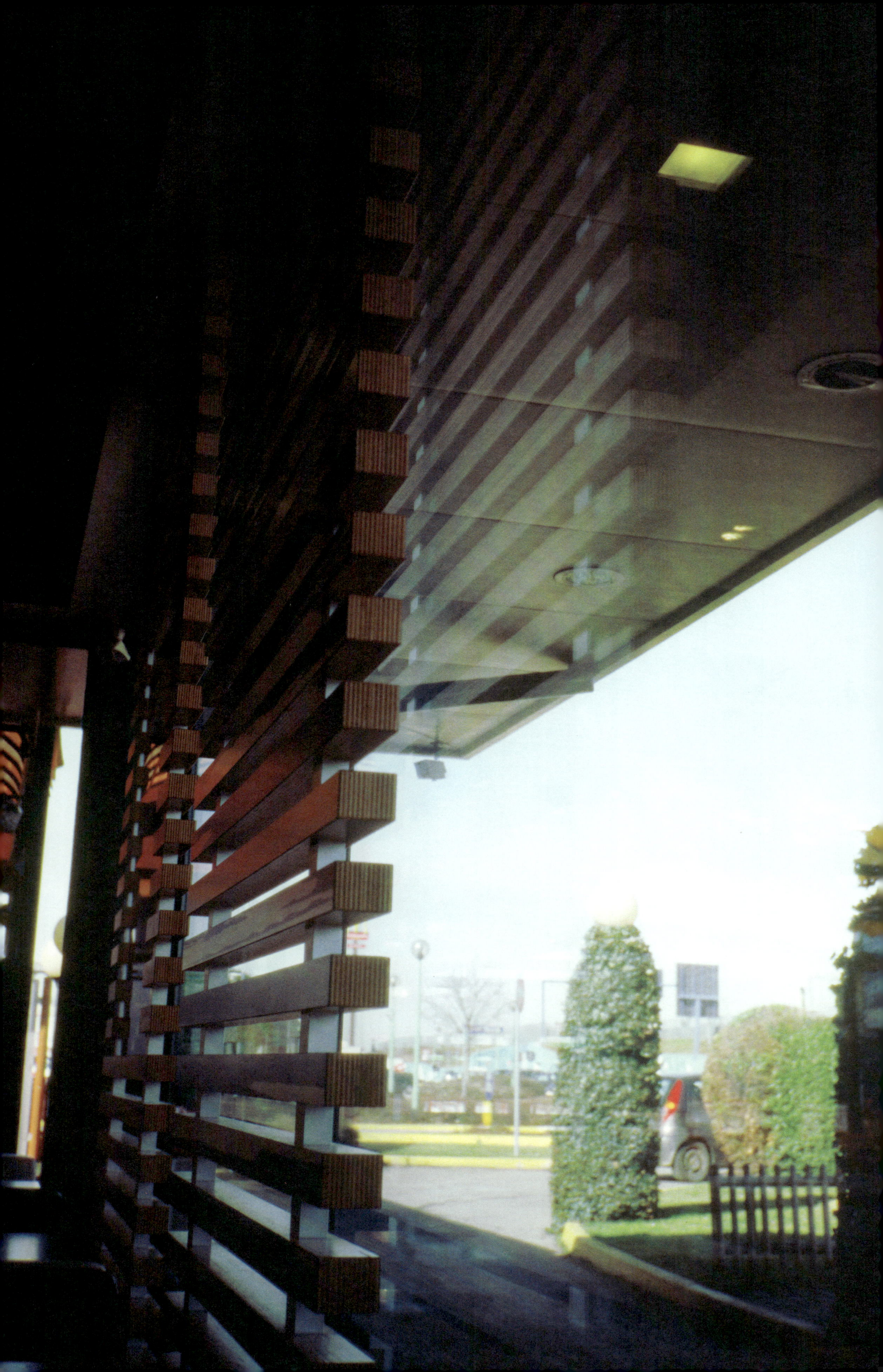

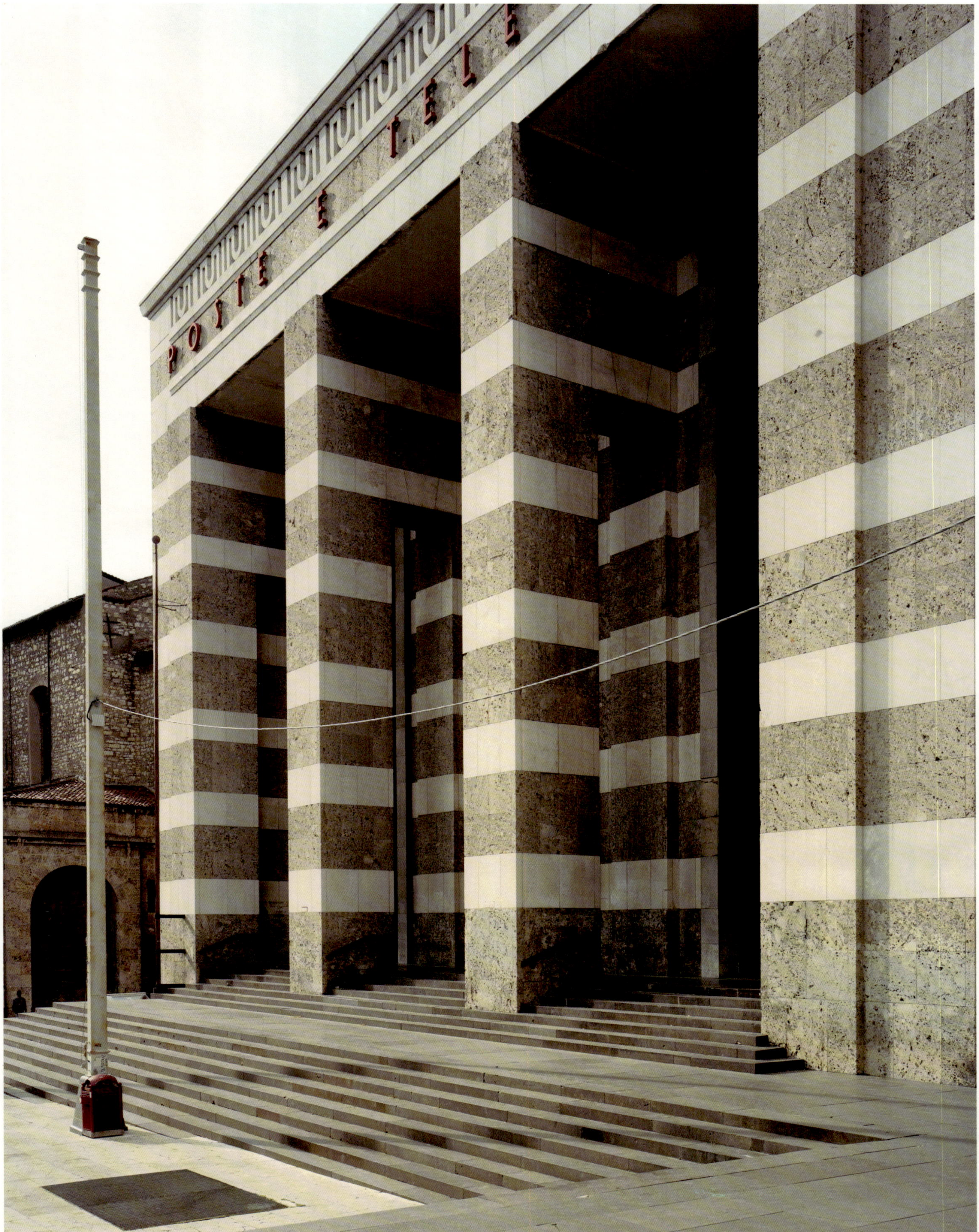
POSTE E TELE

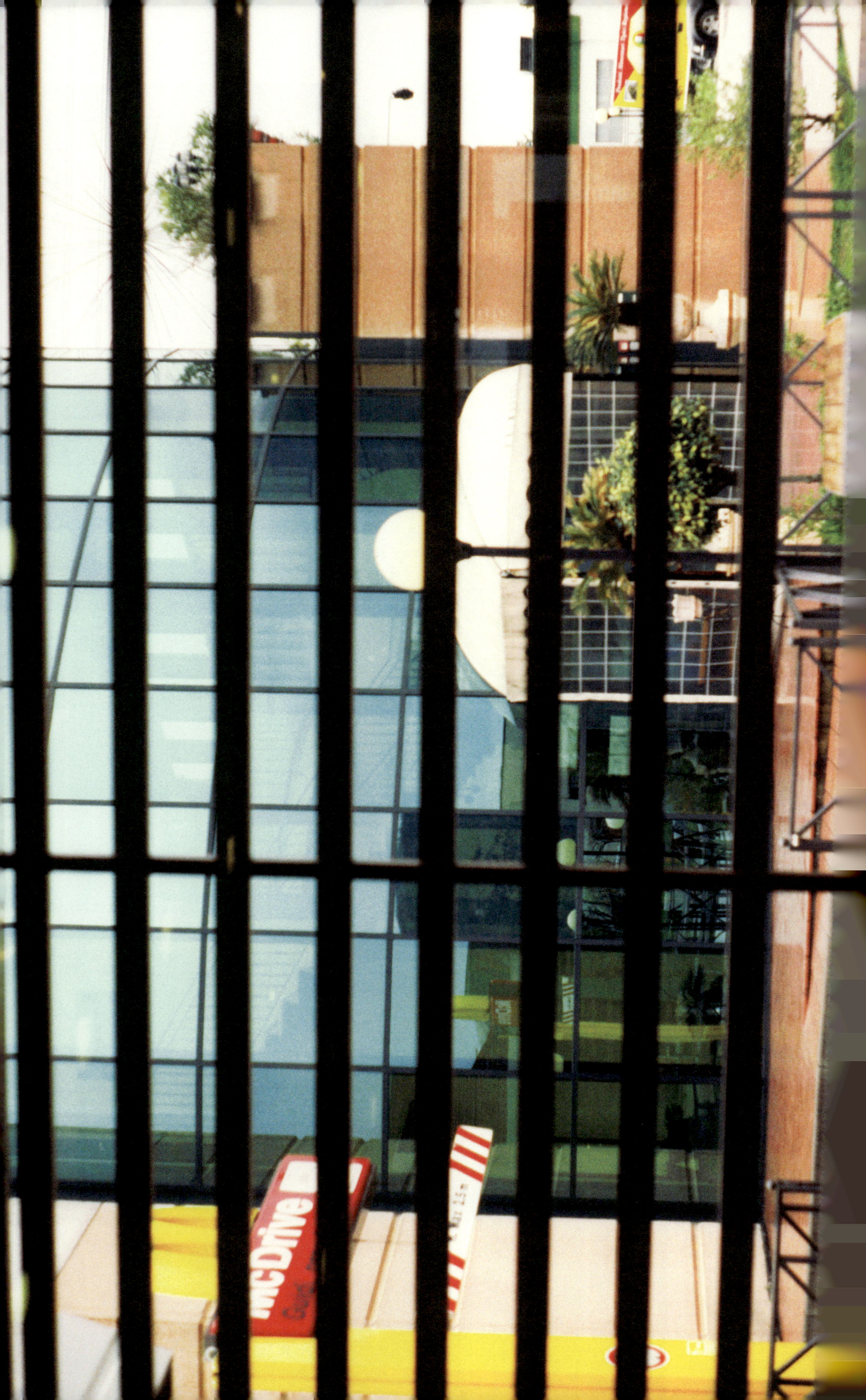
McDrive

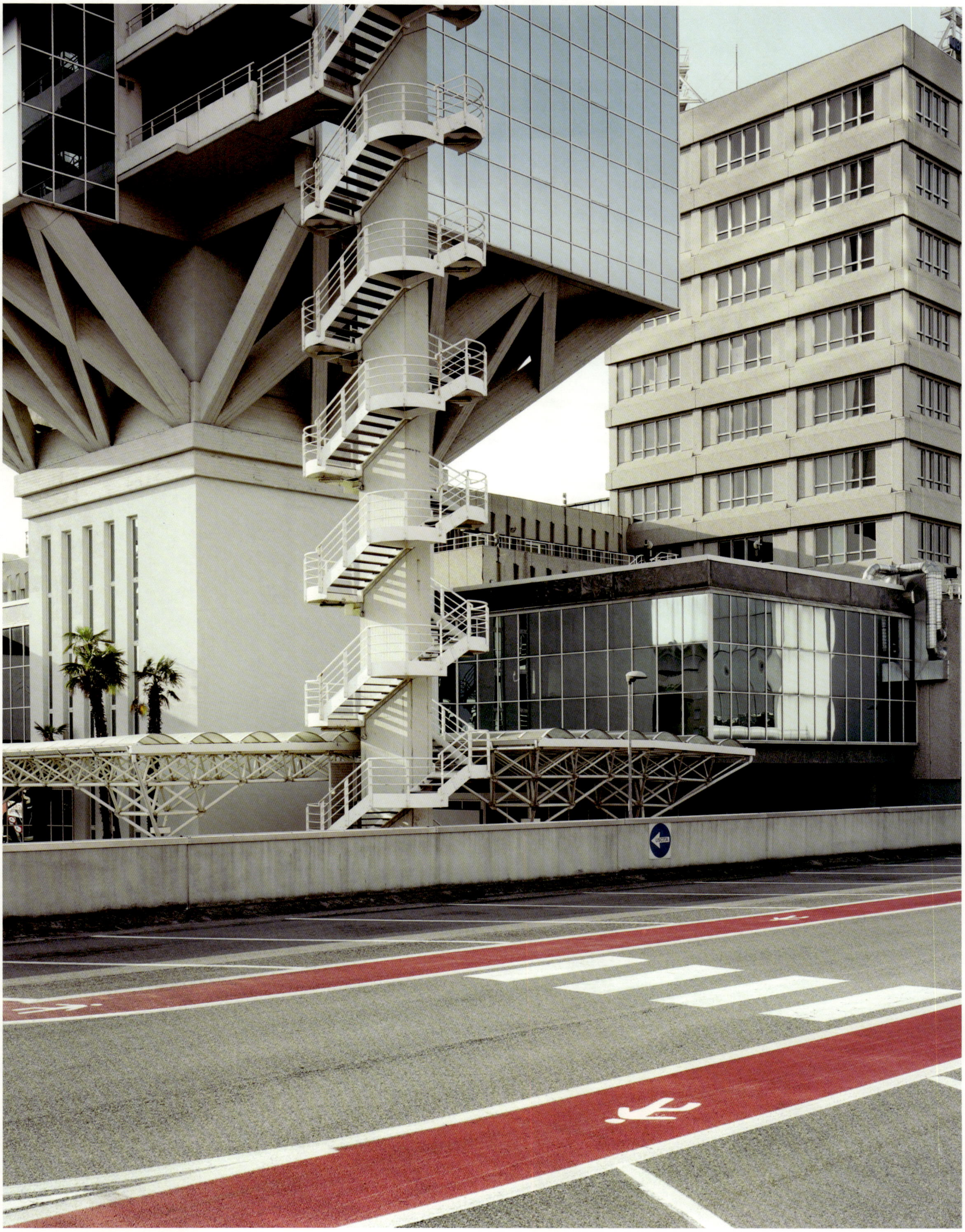

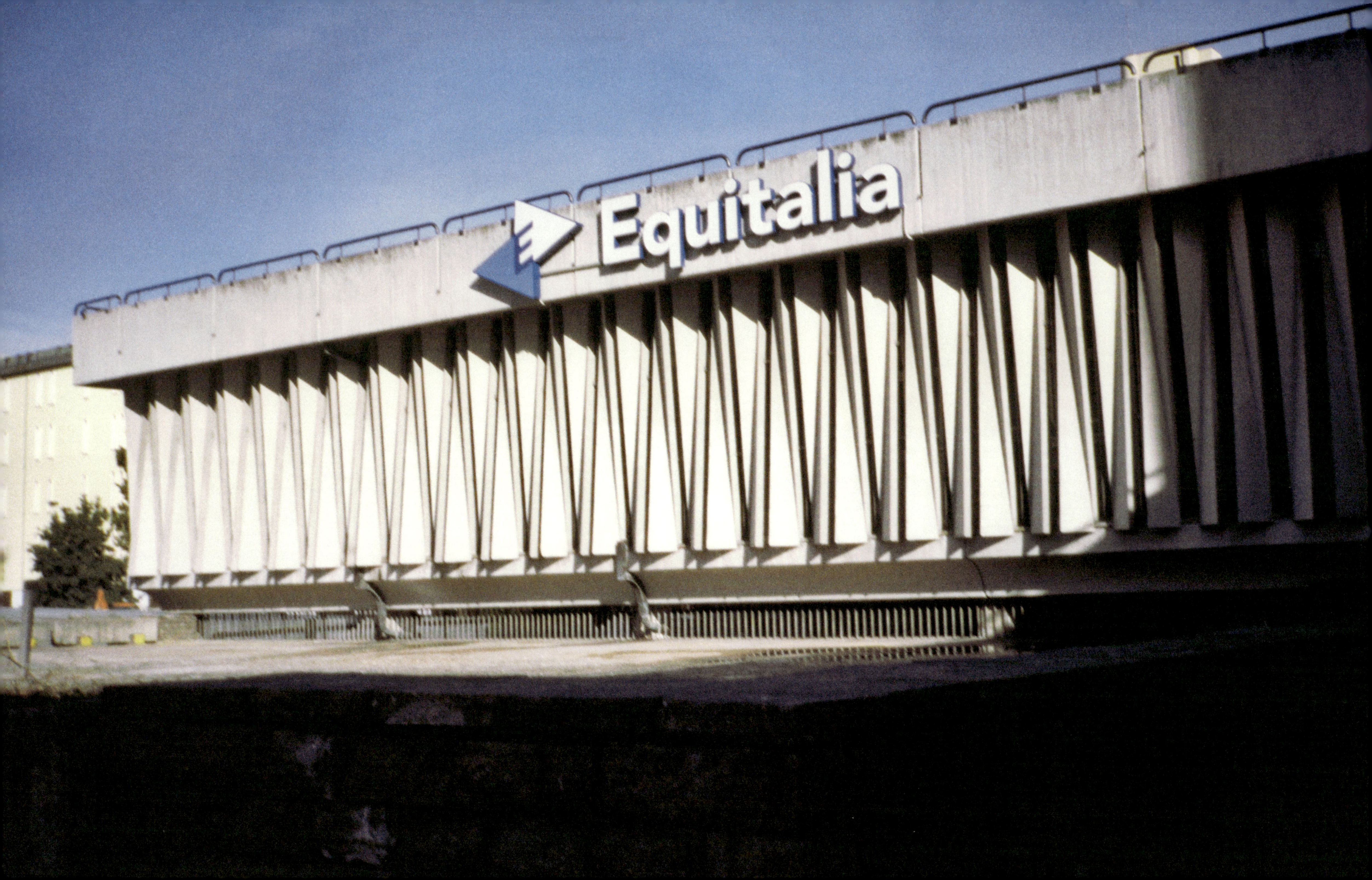
Equitalia

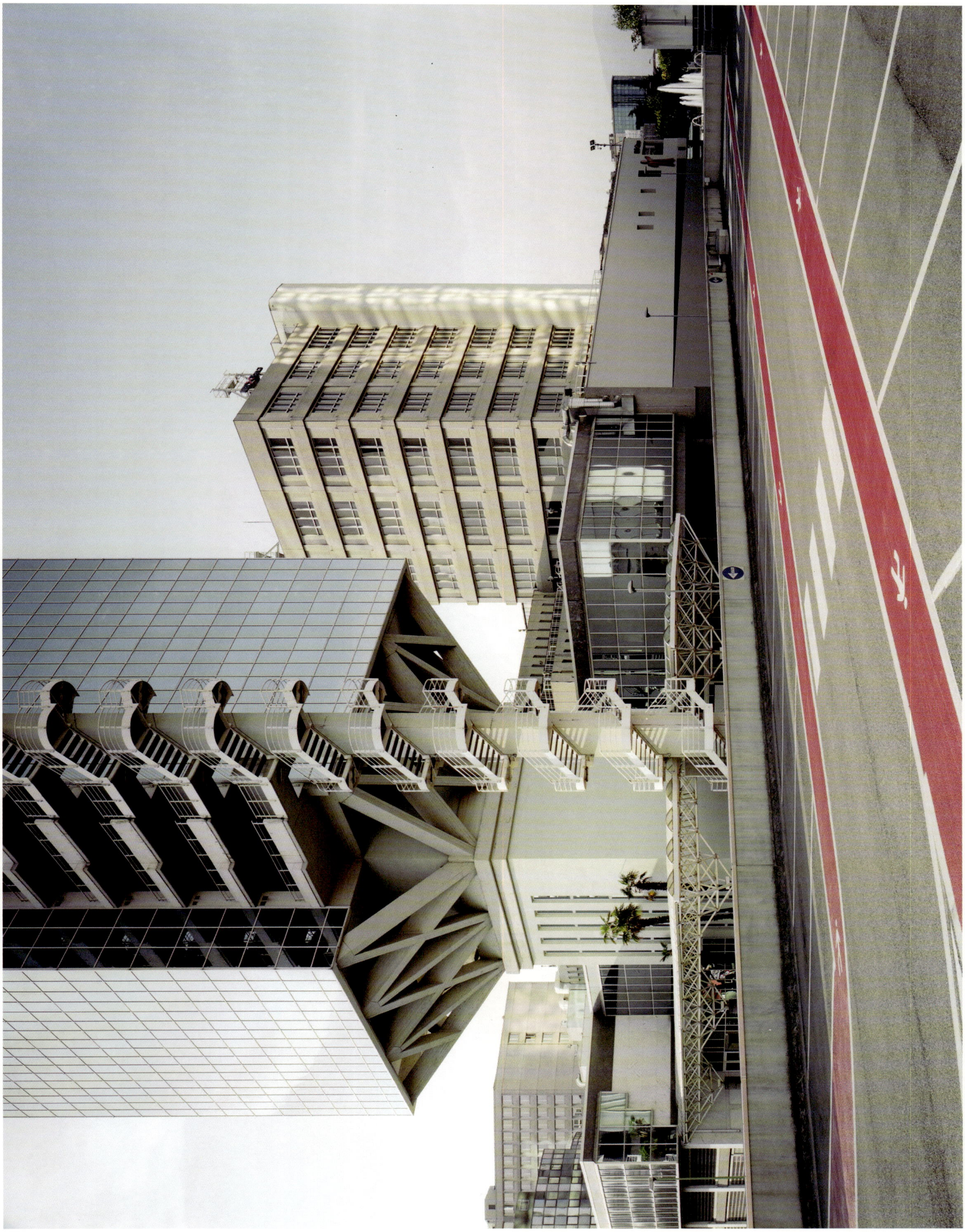

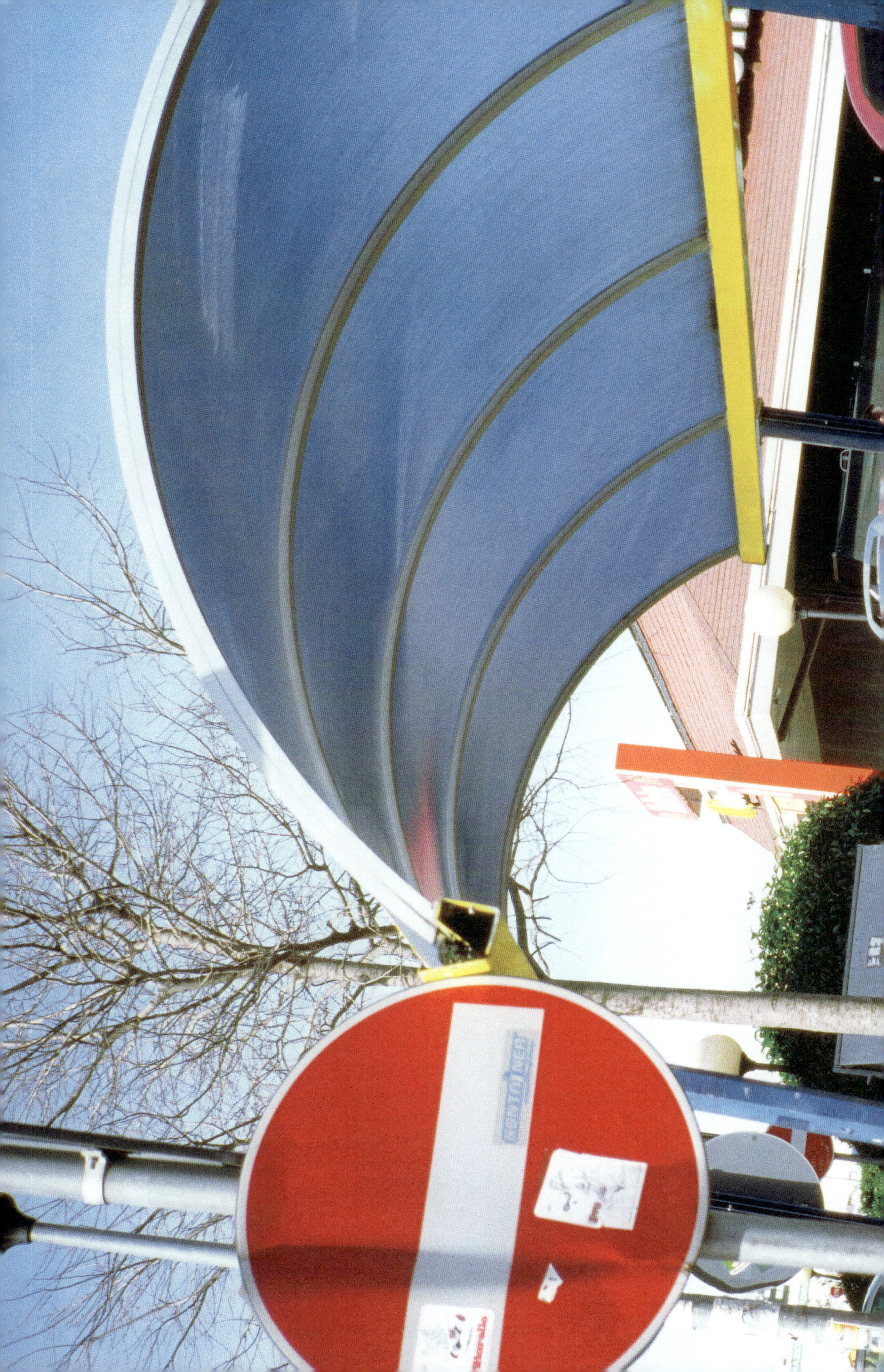

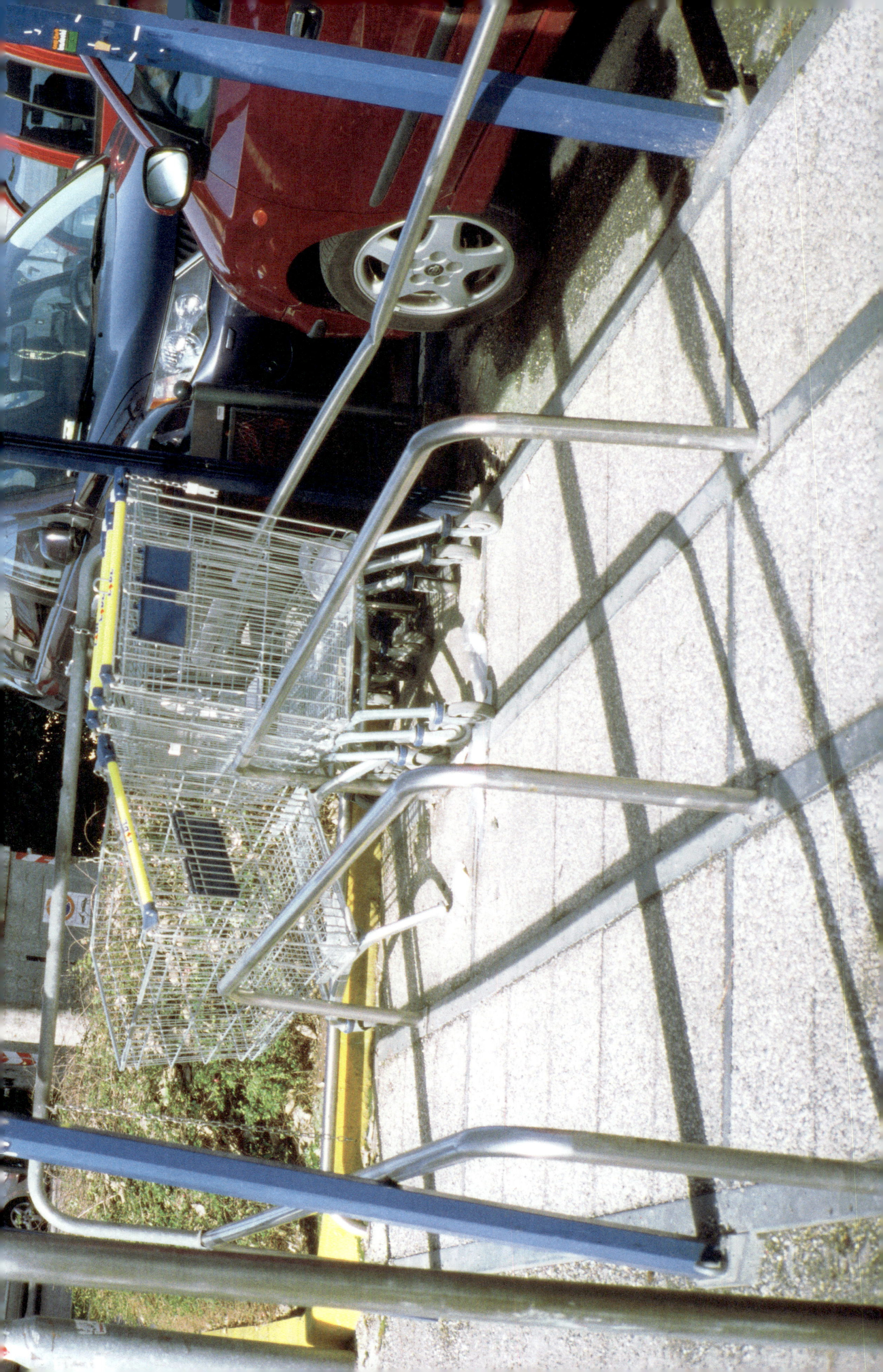

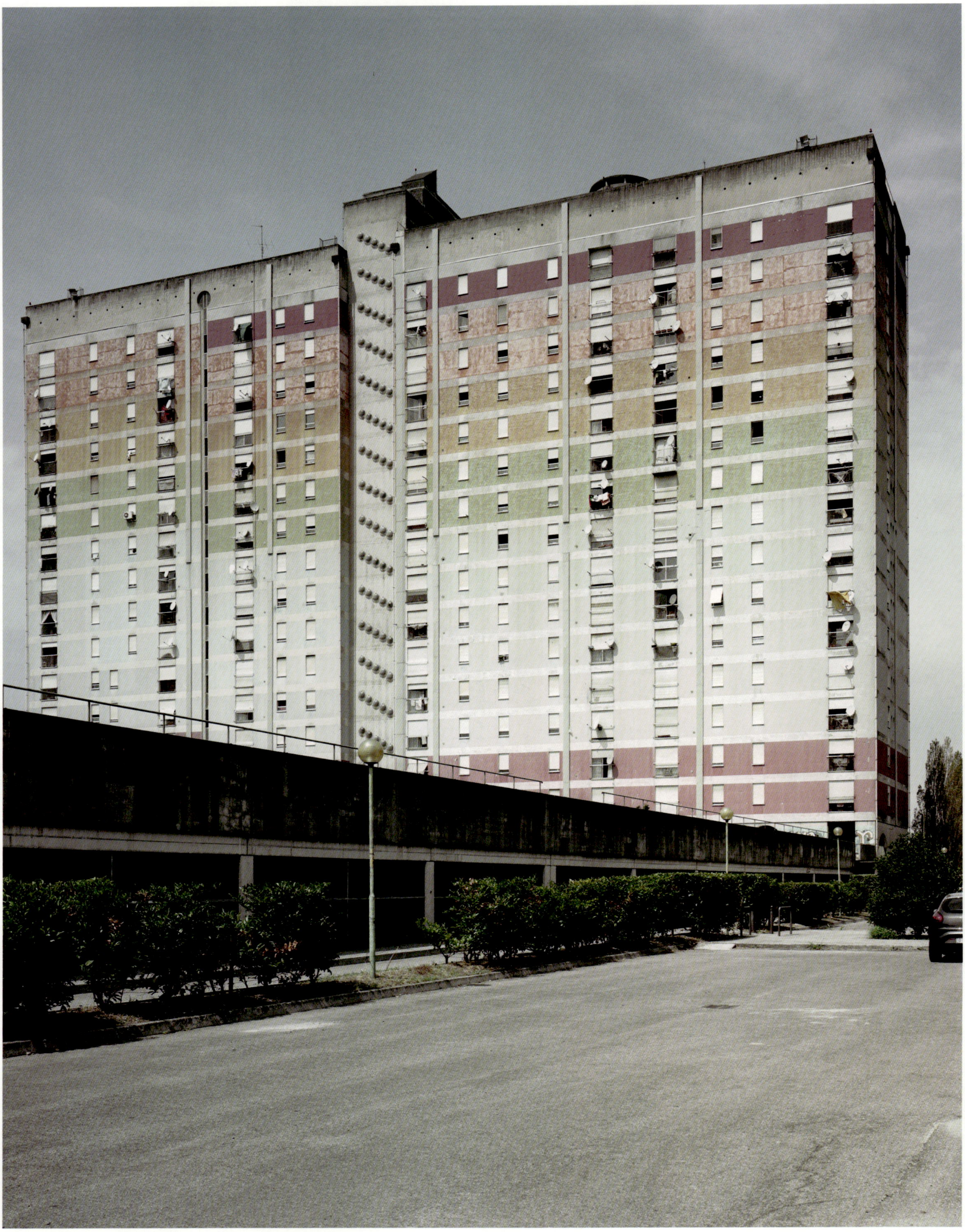

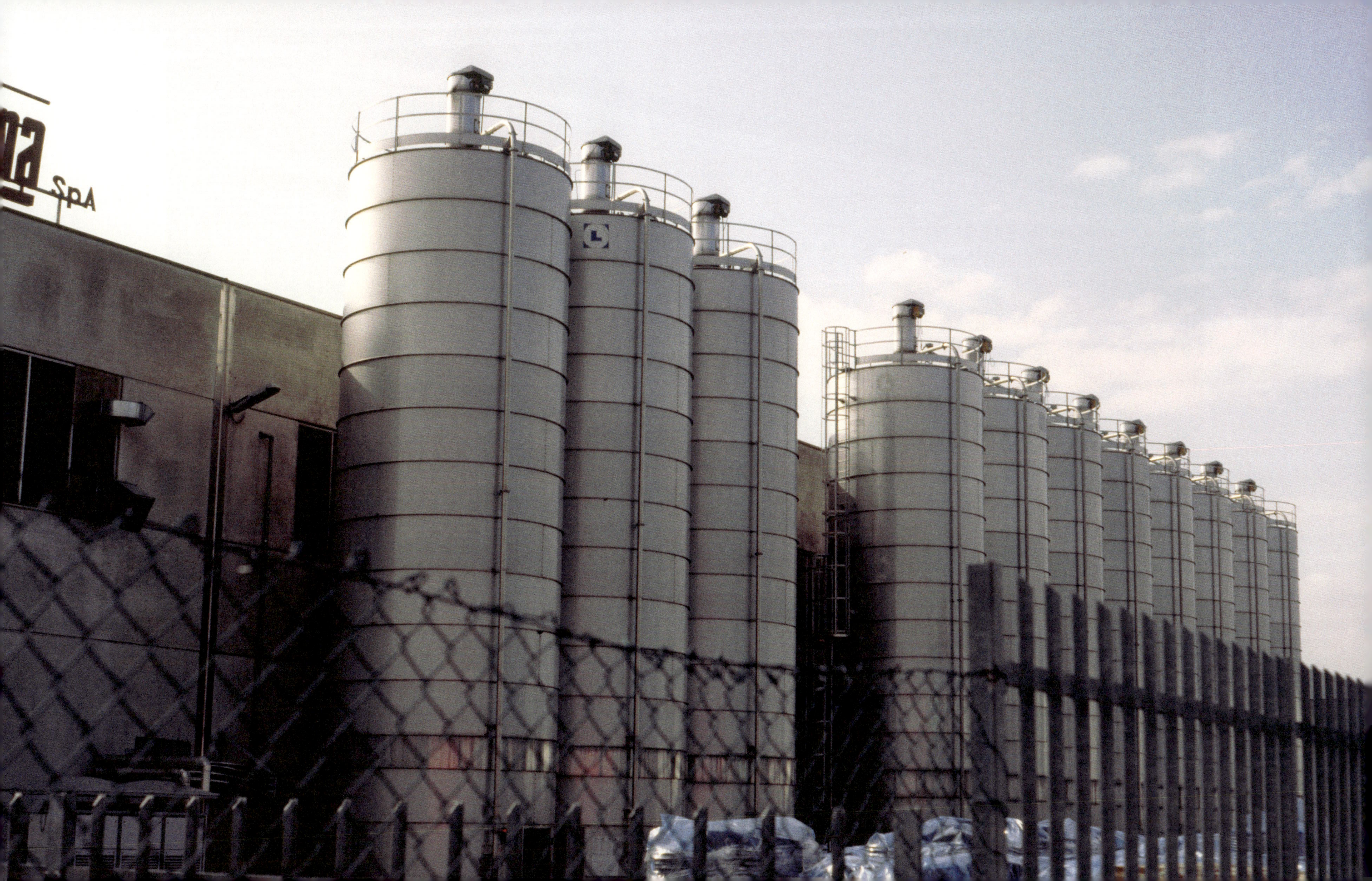
SpA

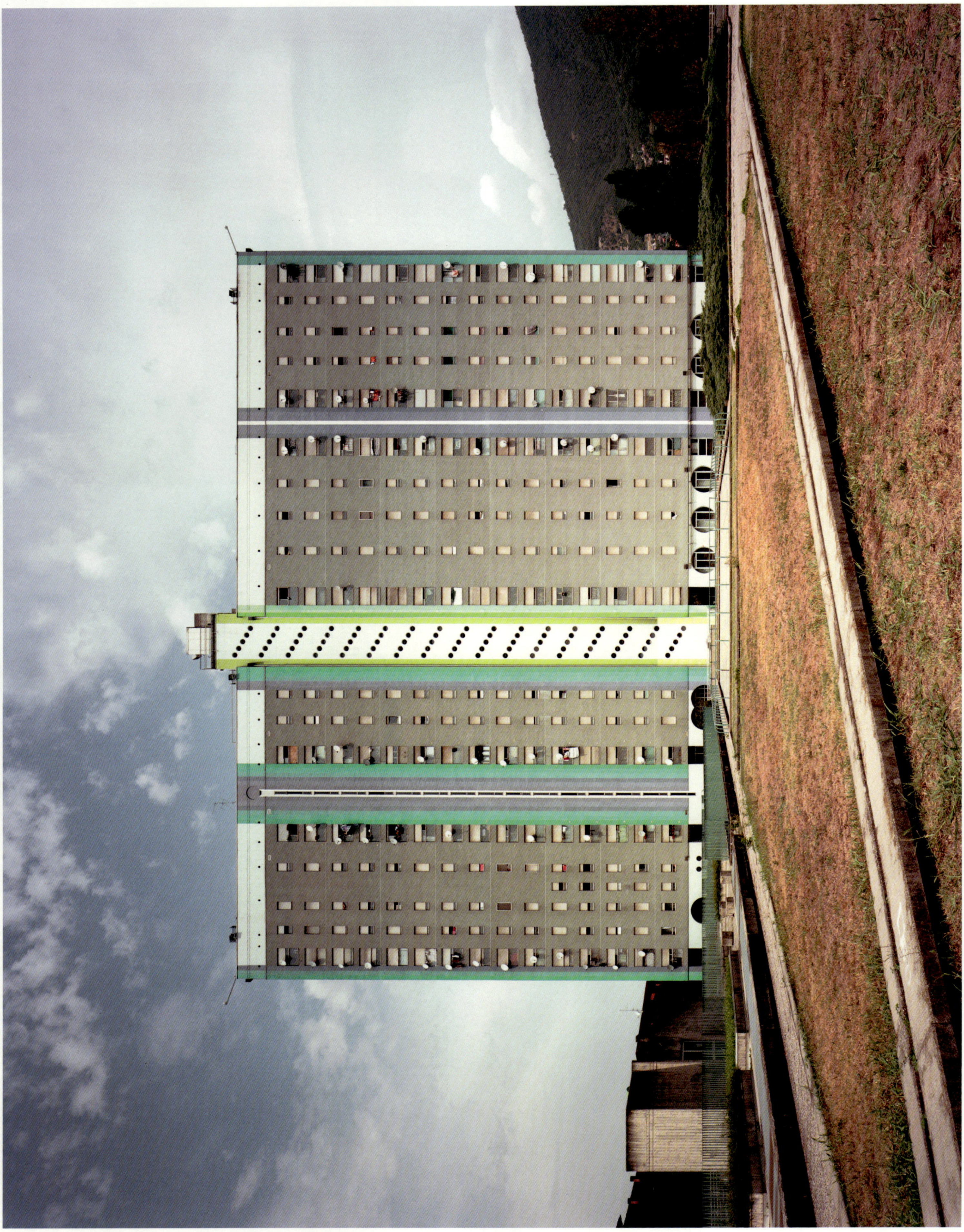

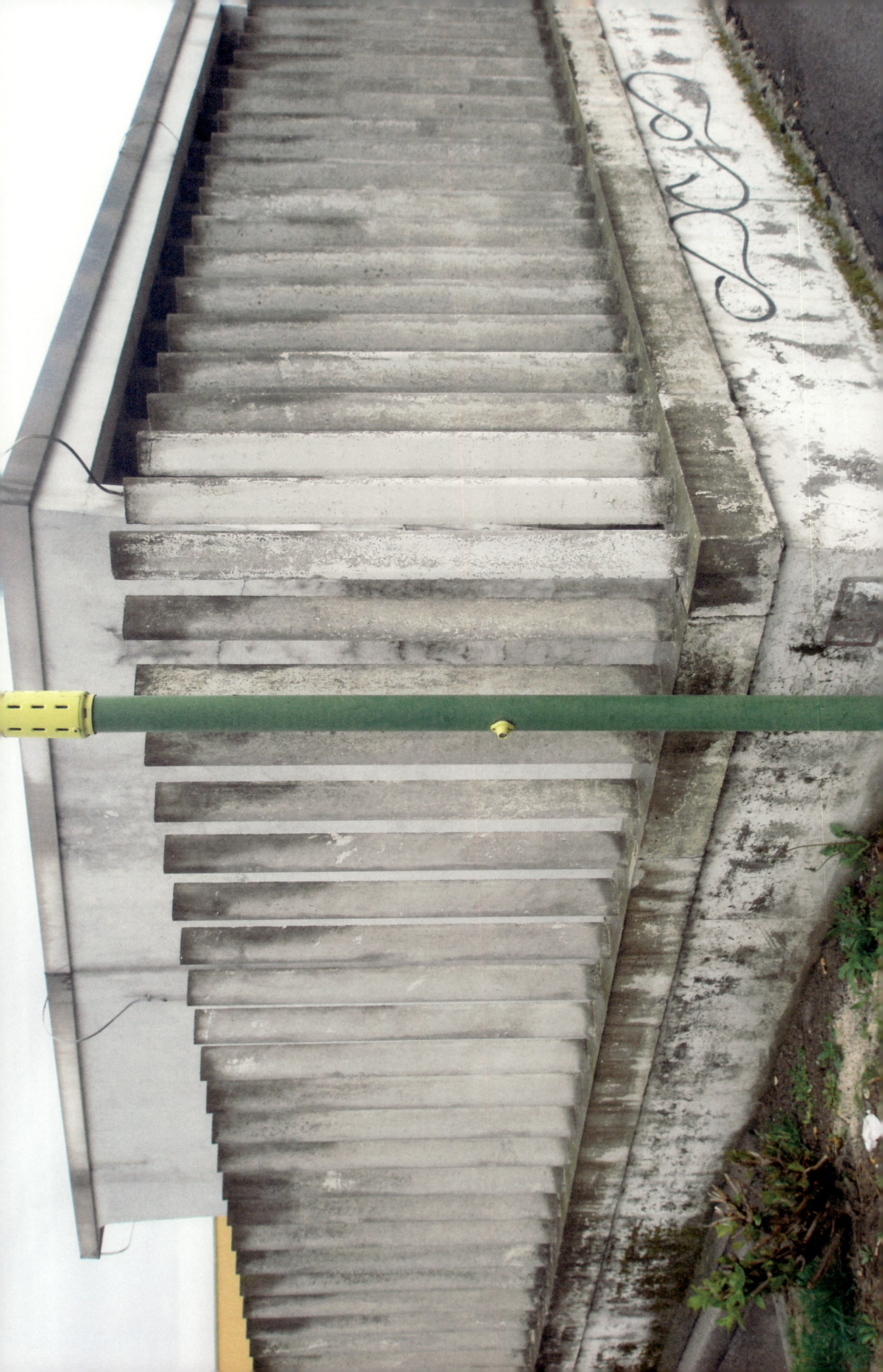

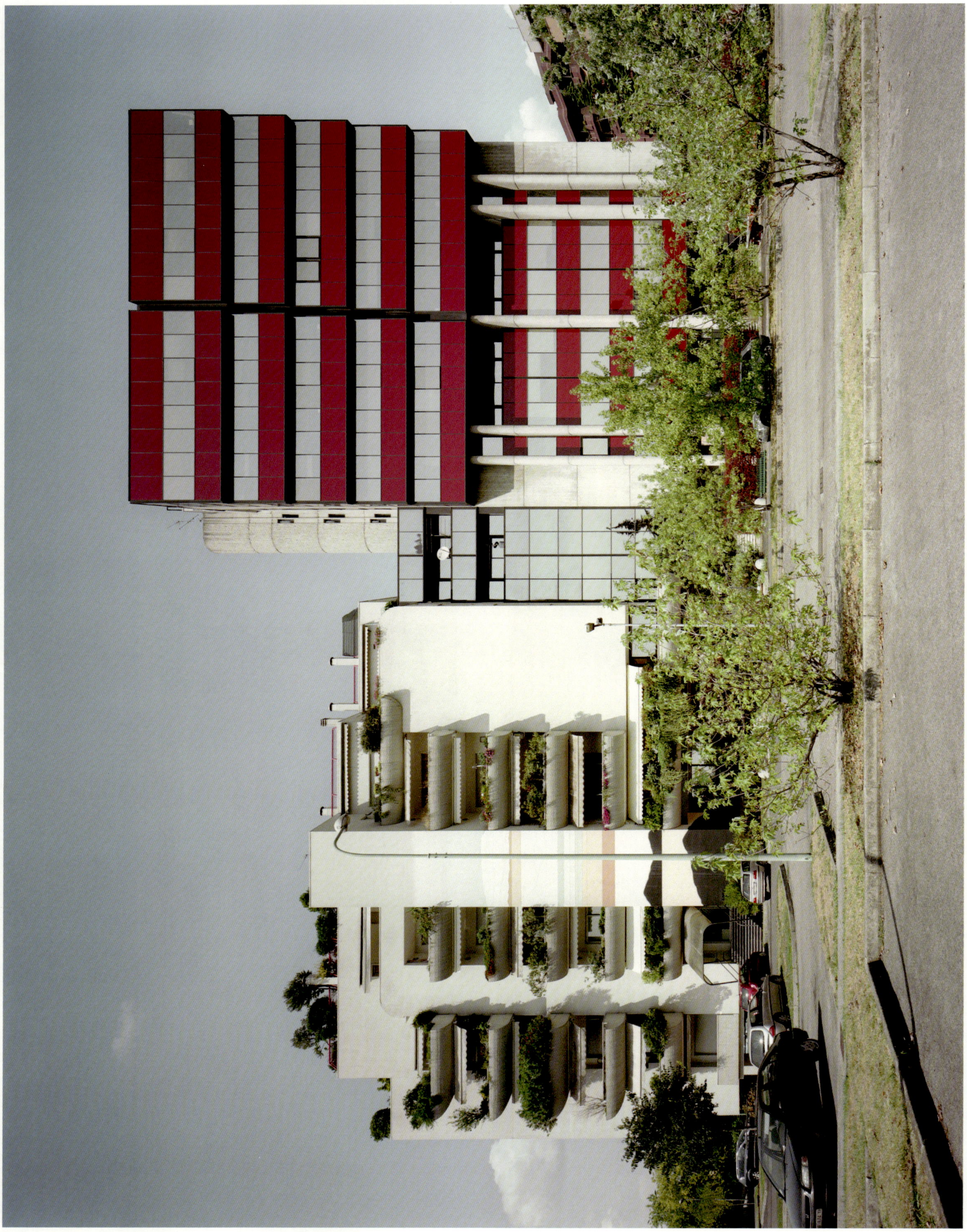

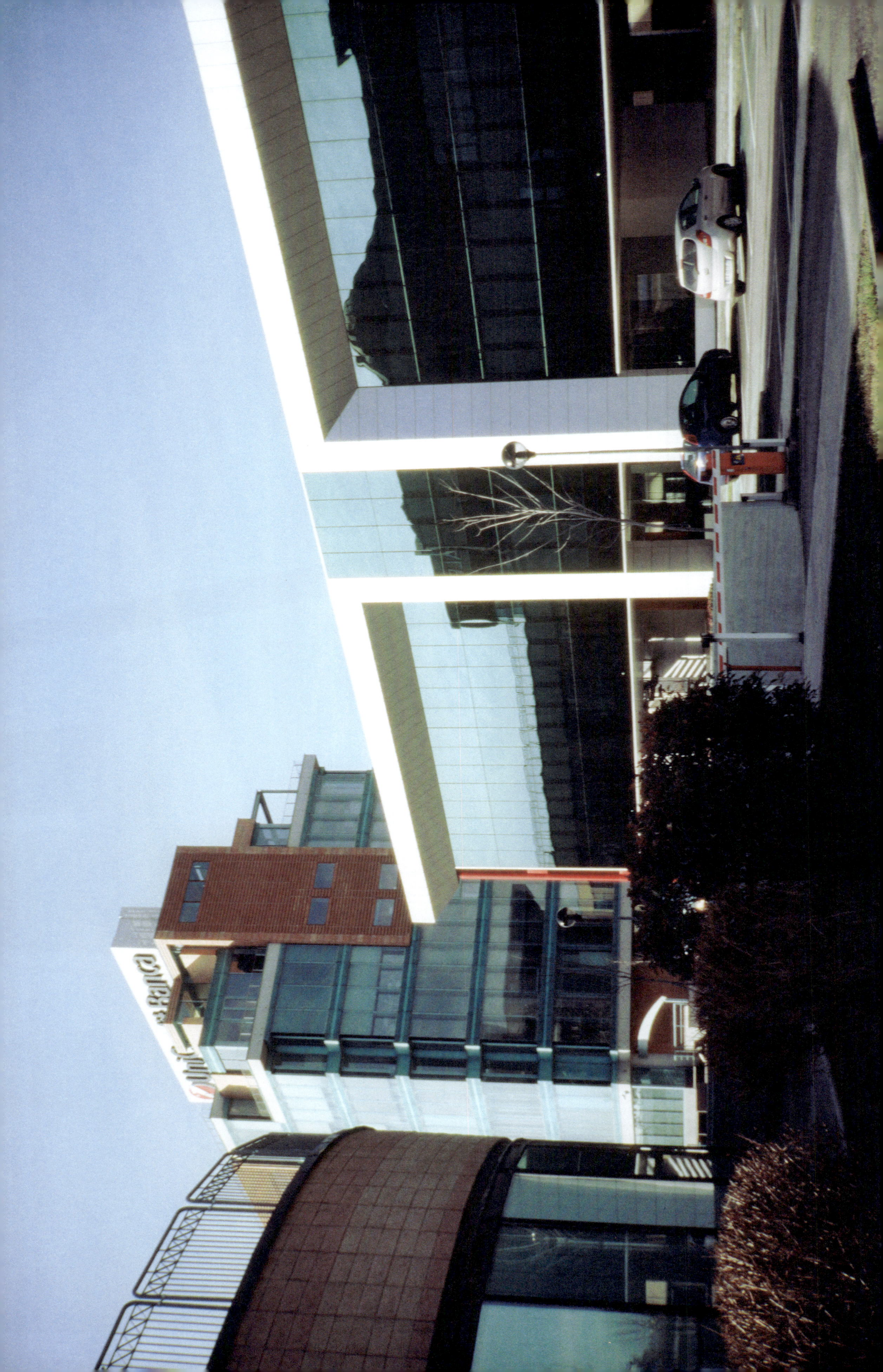

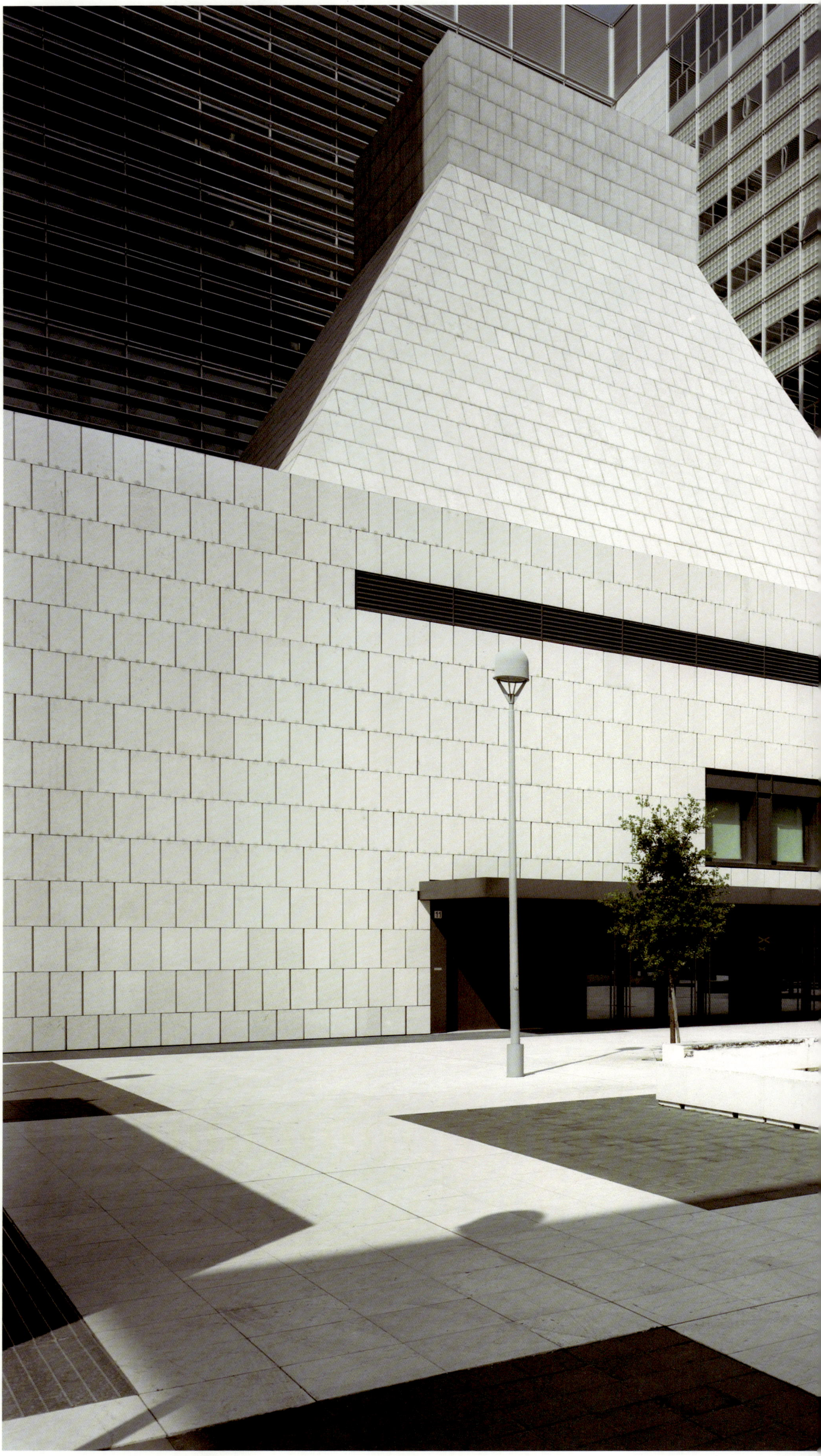

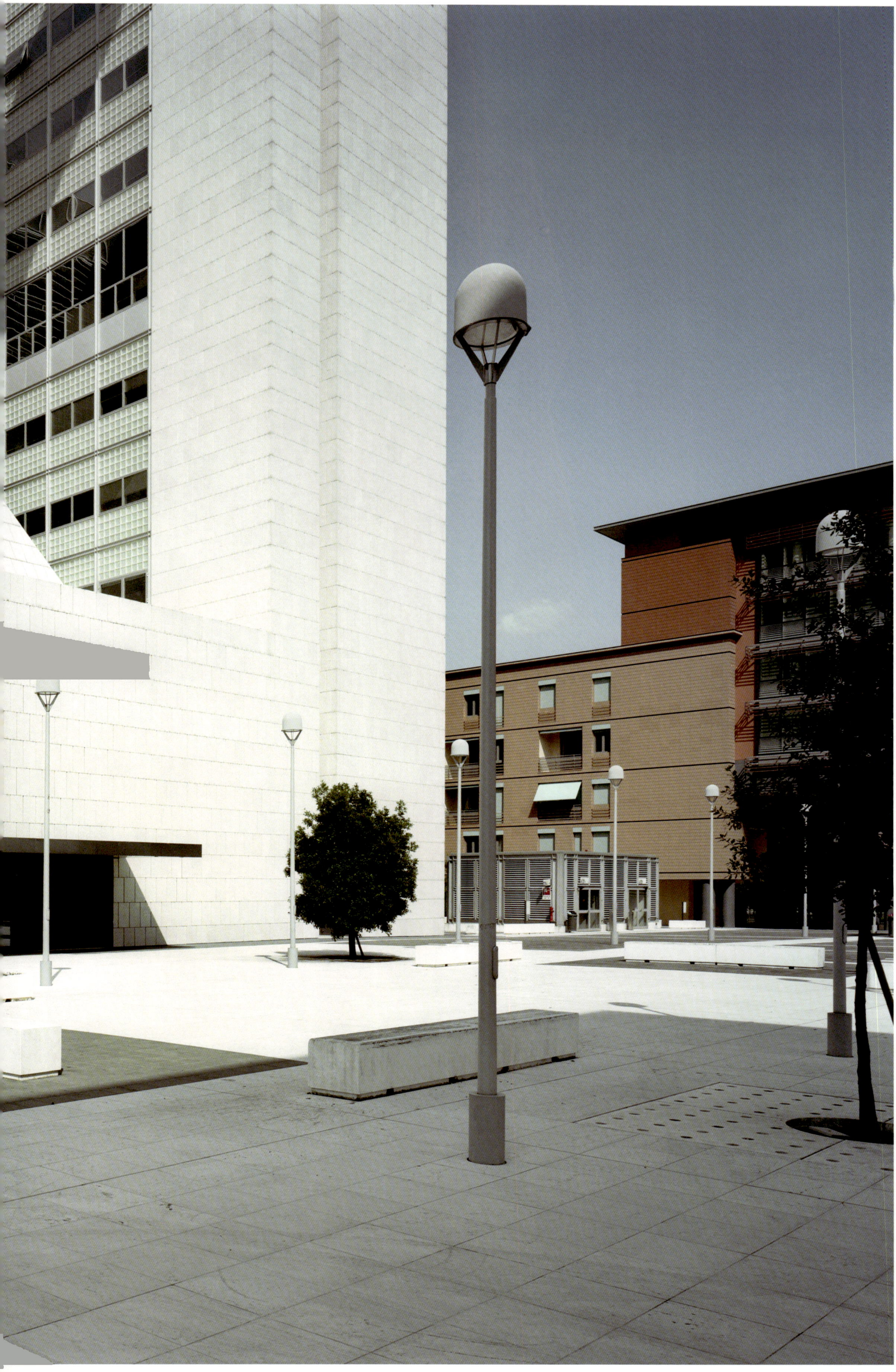

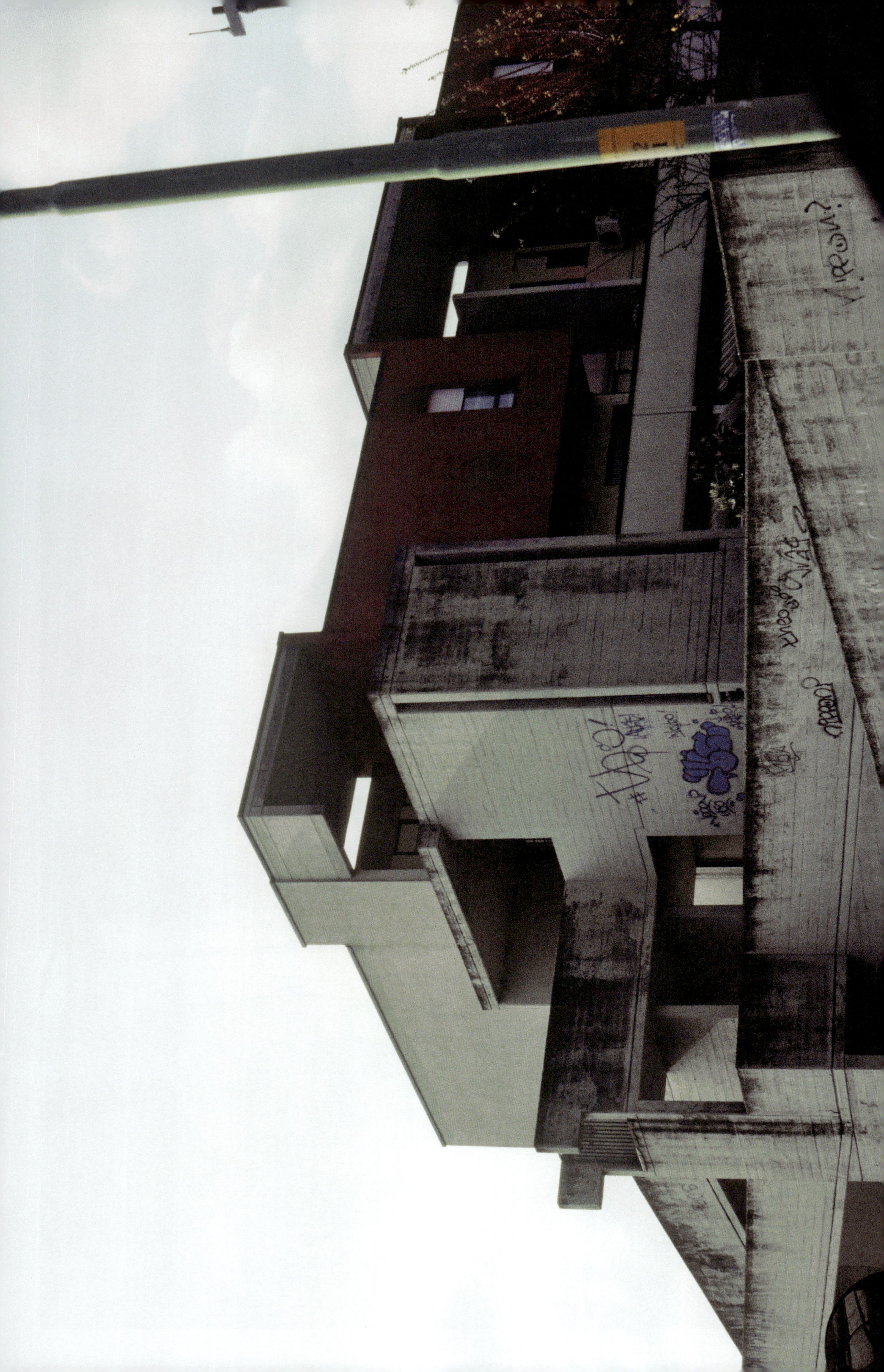

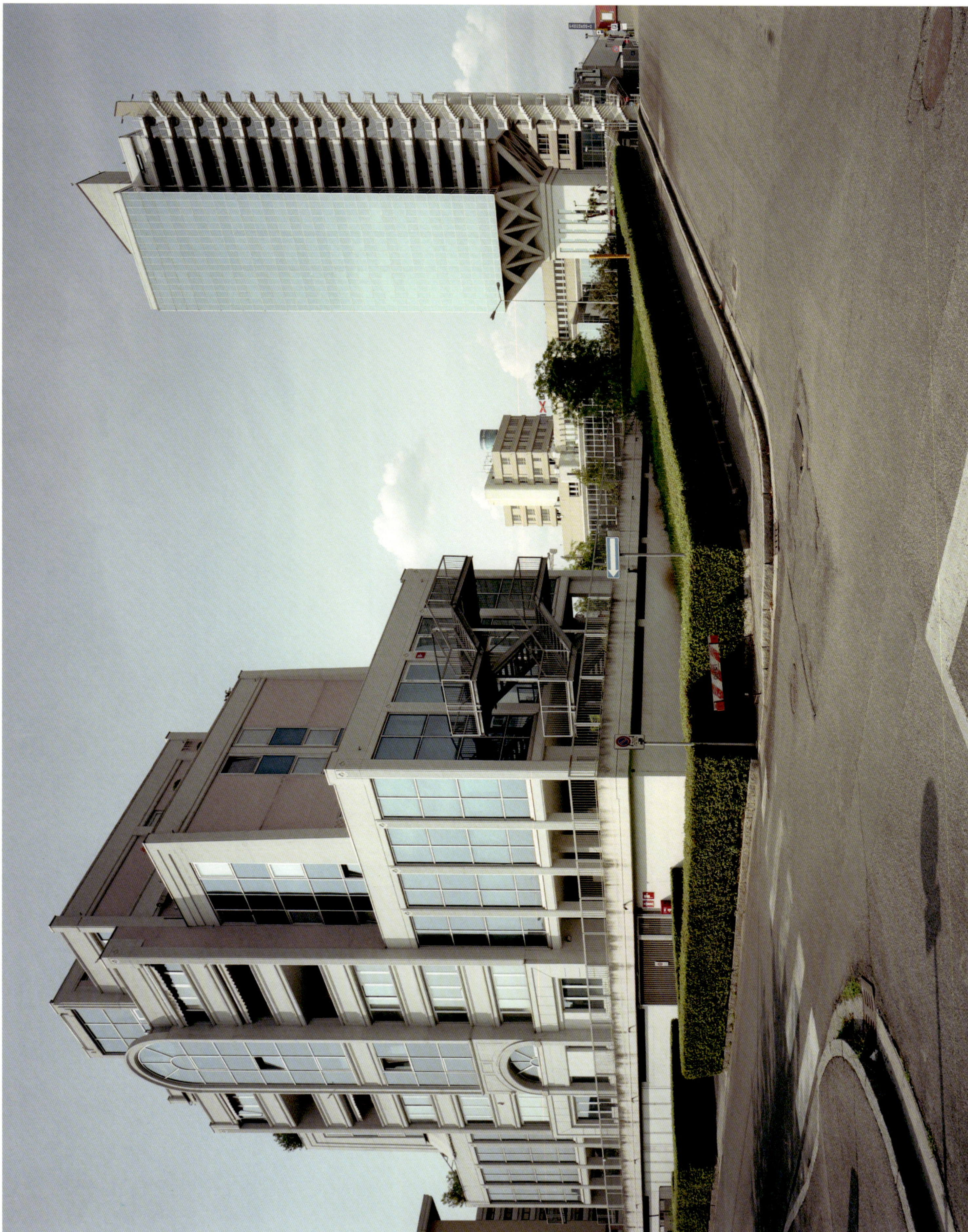

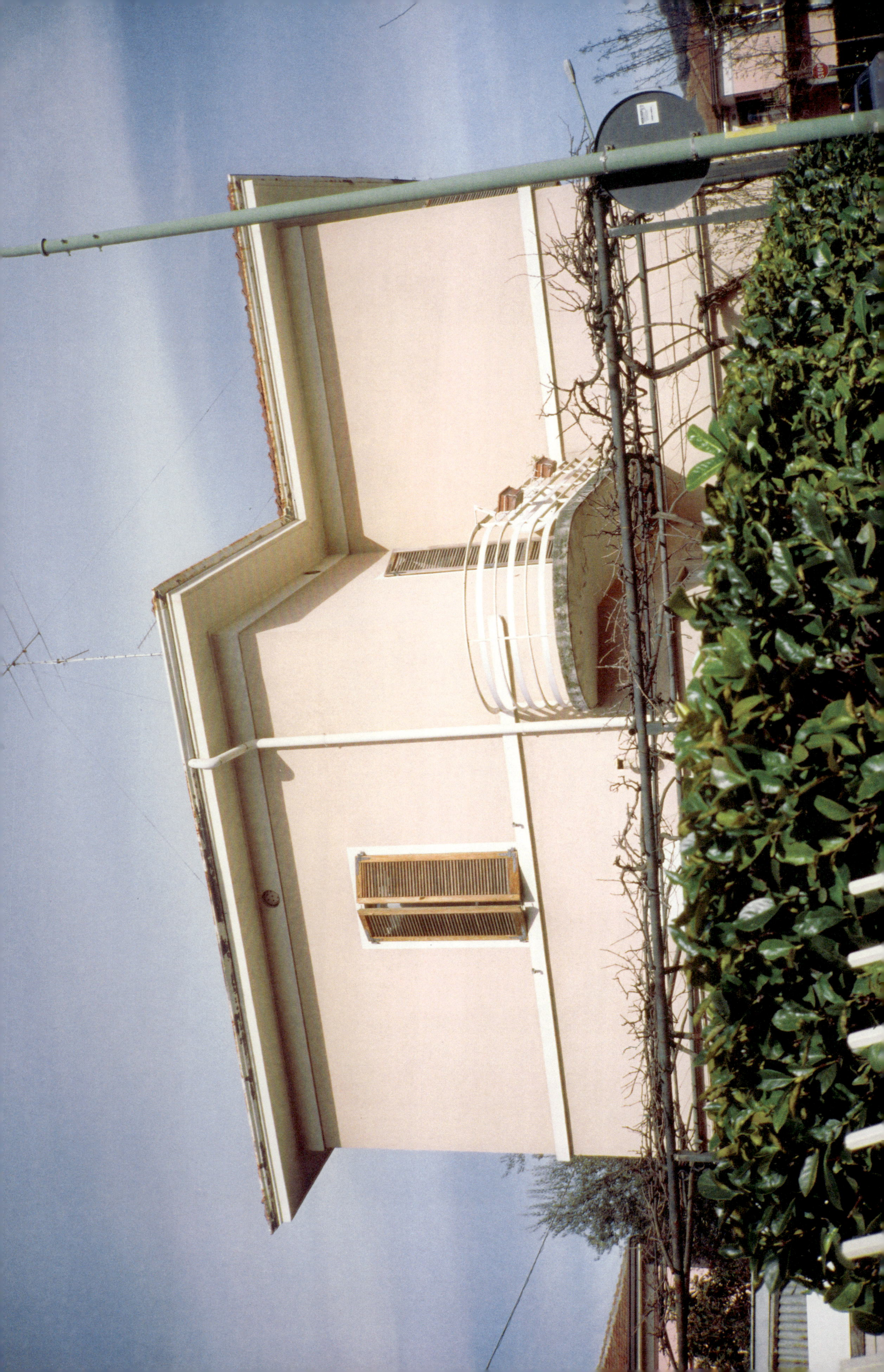

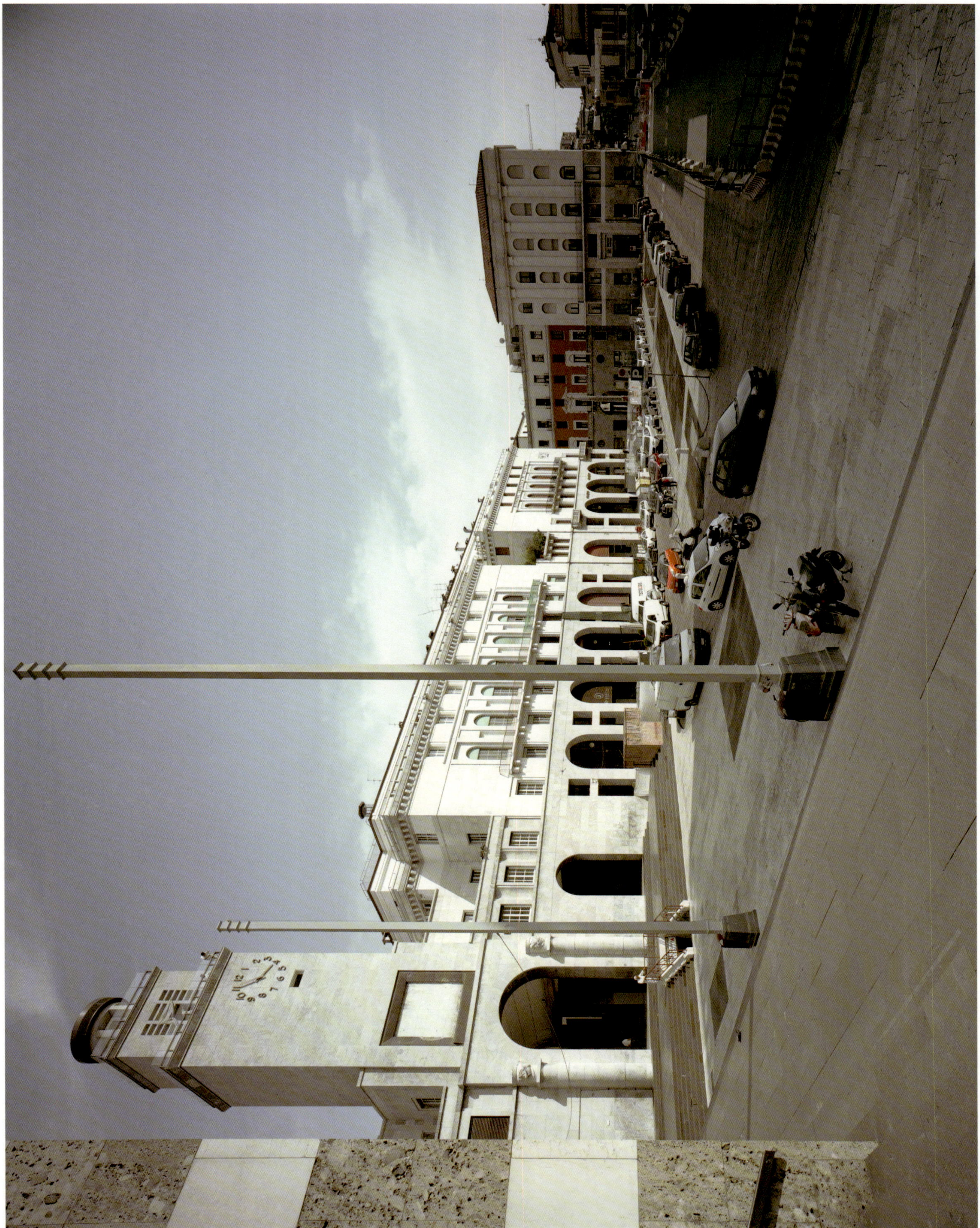

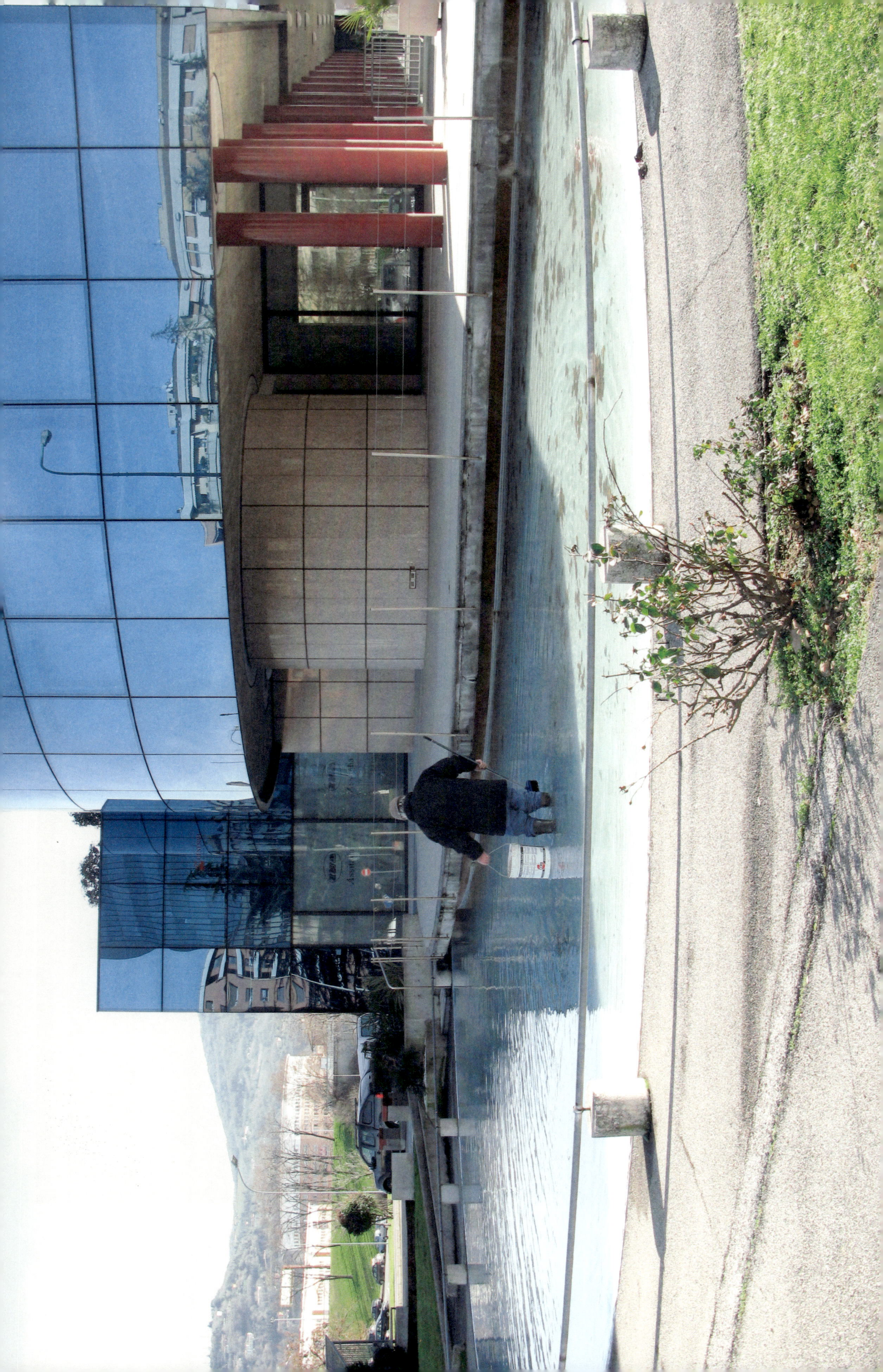

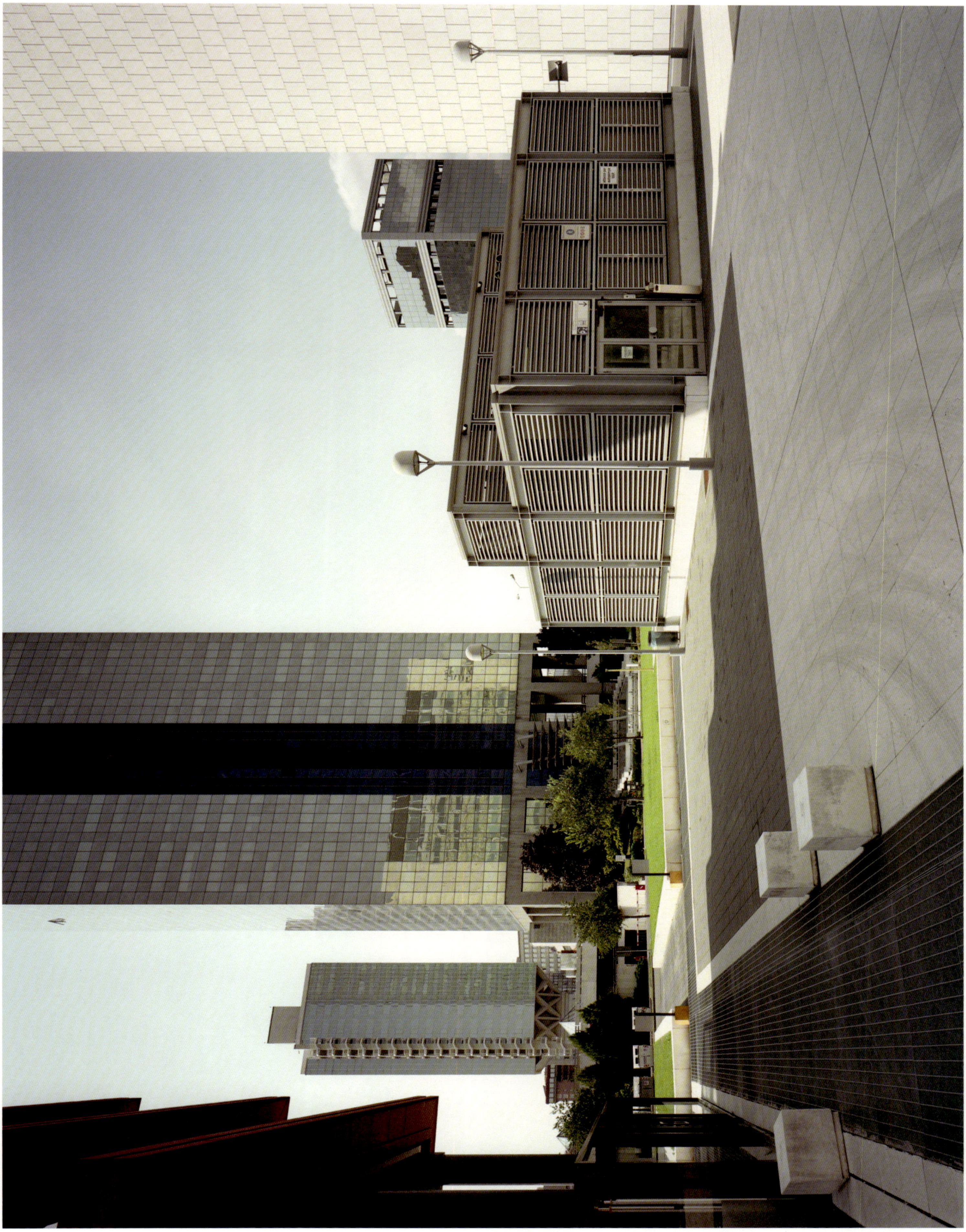

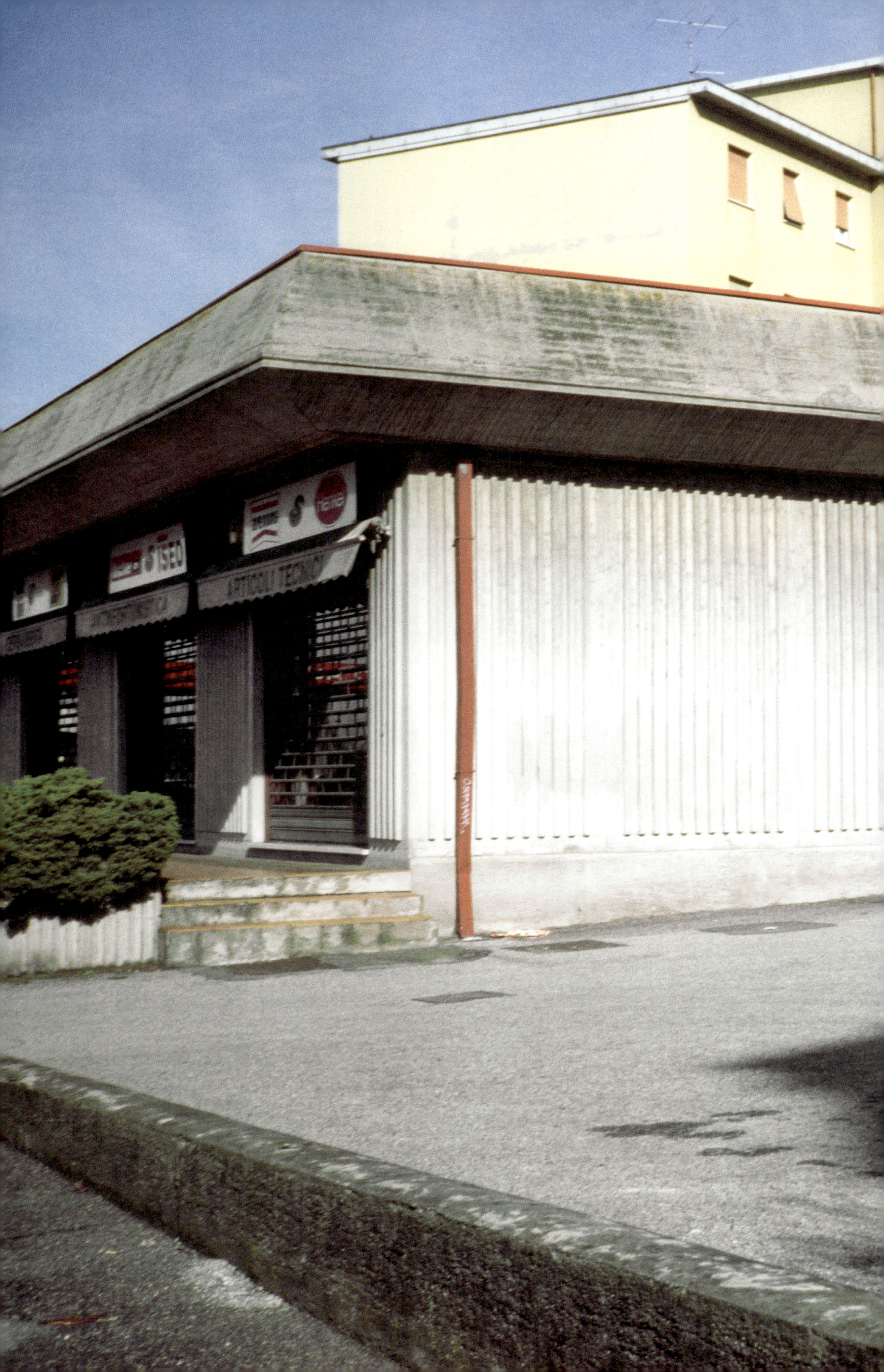
ISEO

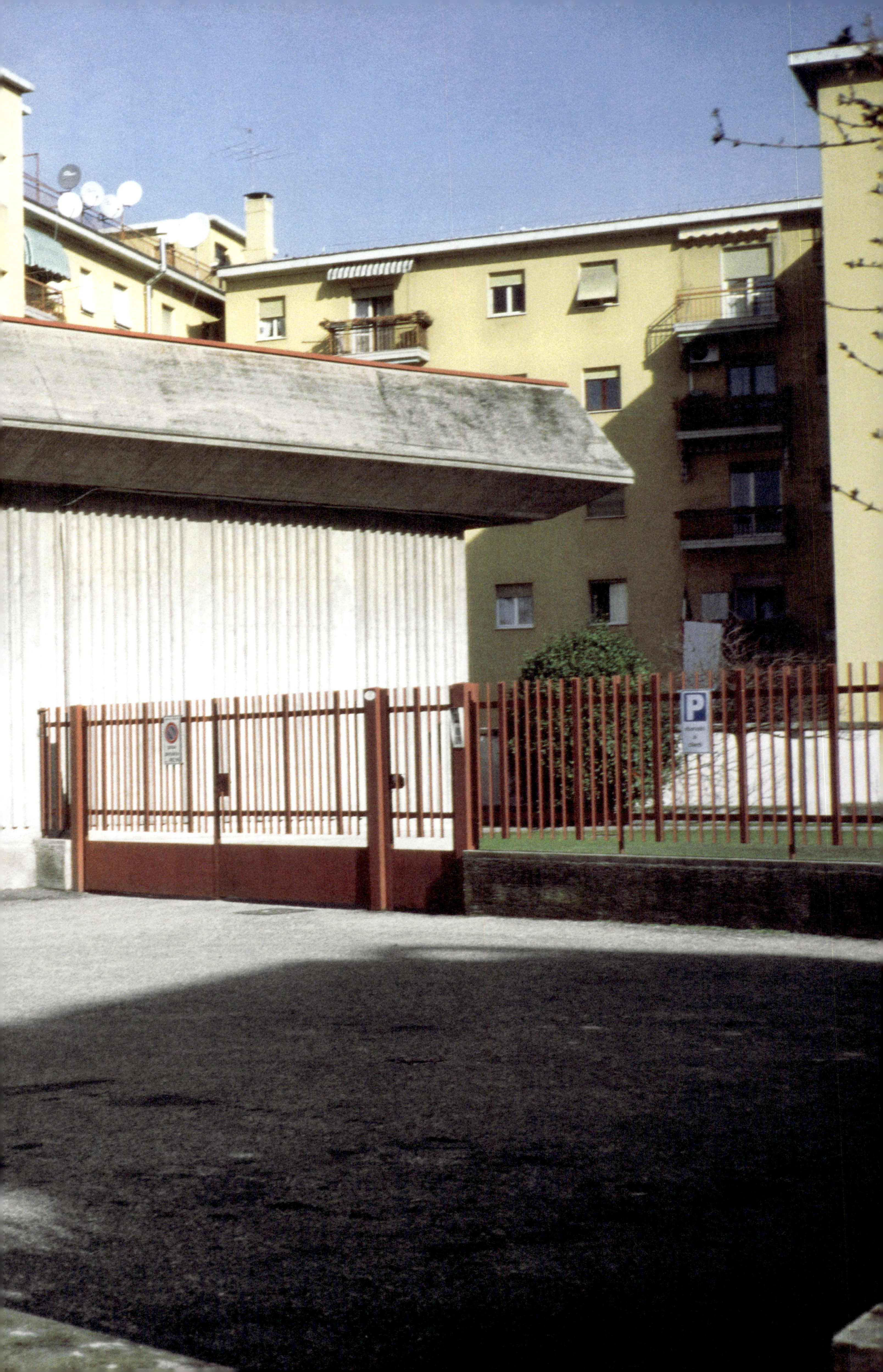
P

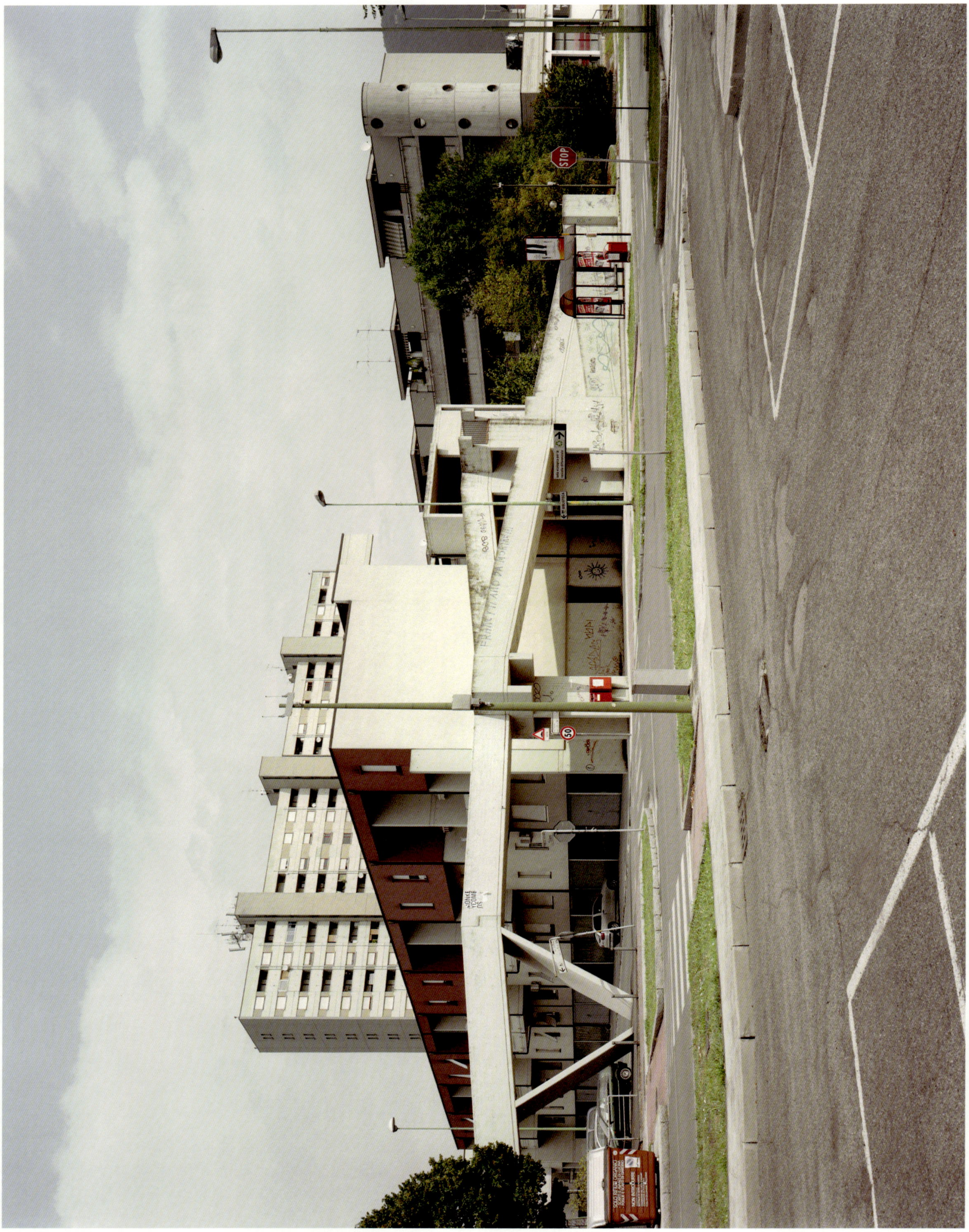
STOP
50

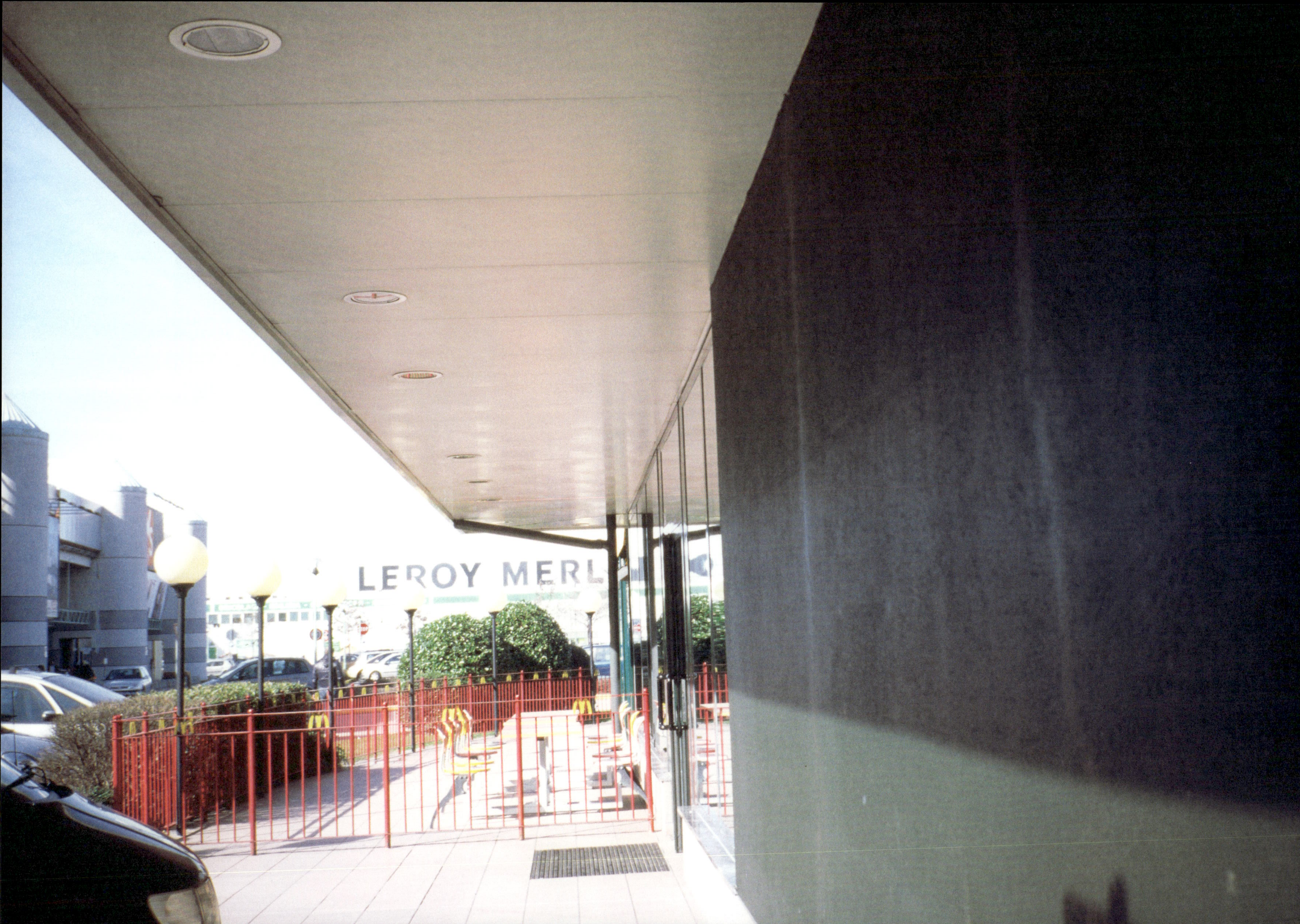
LEROY MERL

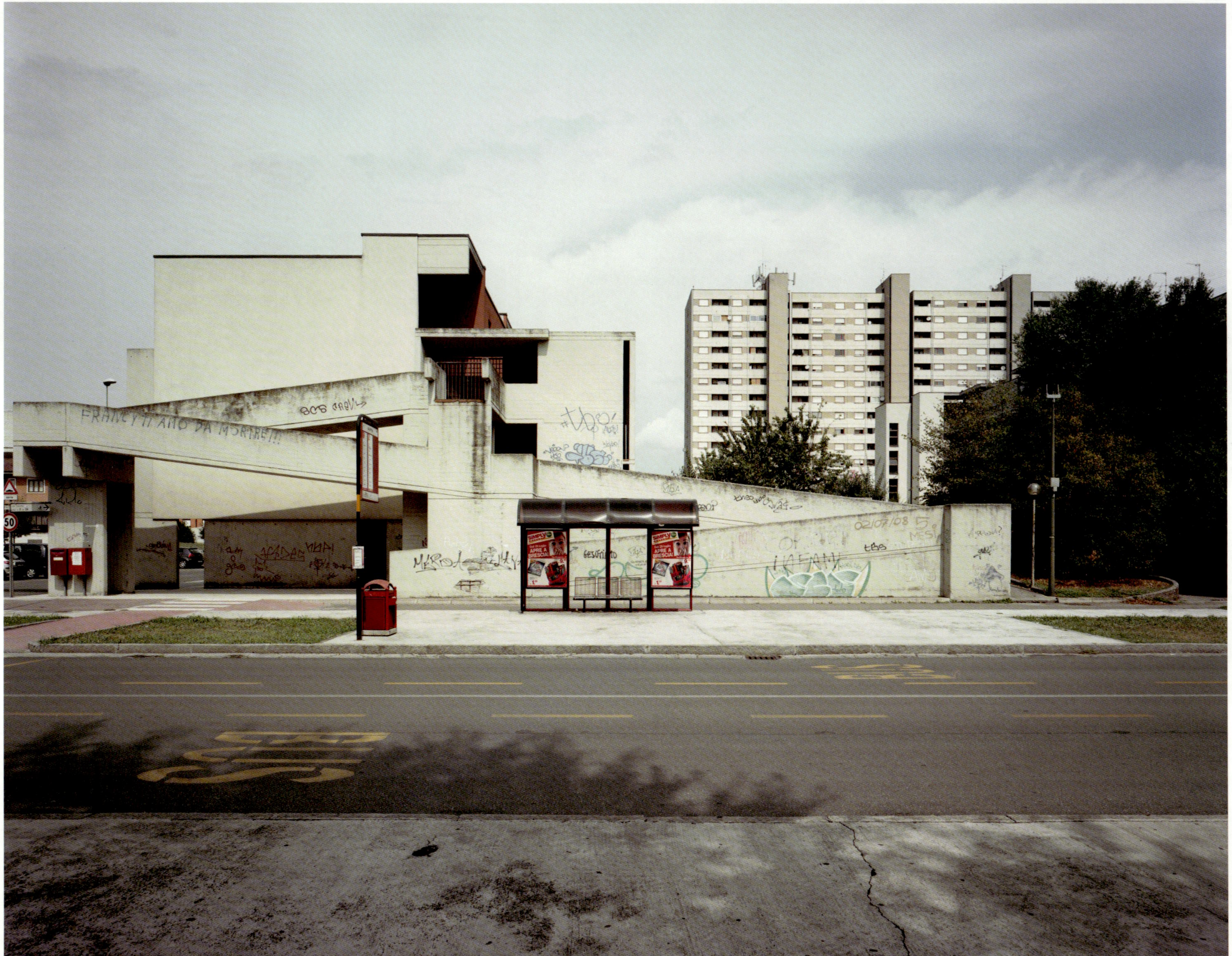
FRANCY TI AMO DA MORIRE!!!
50

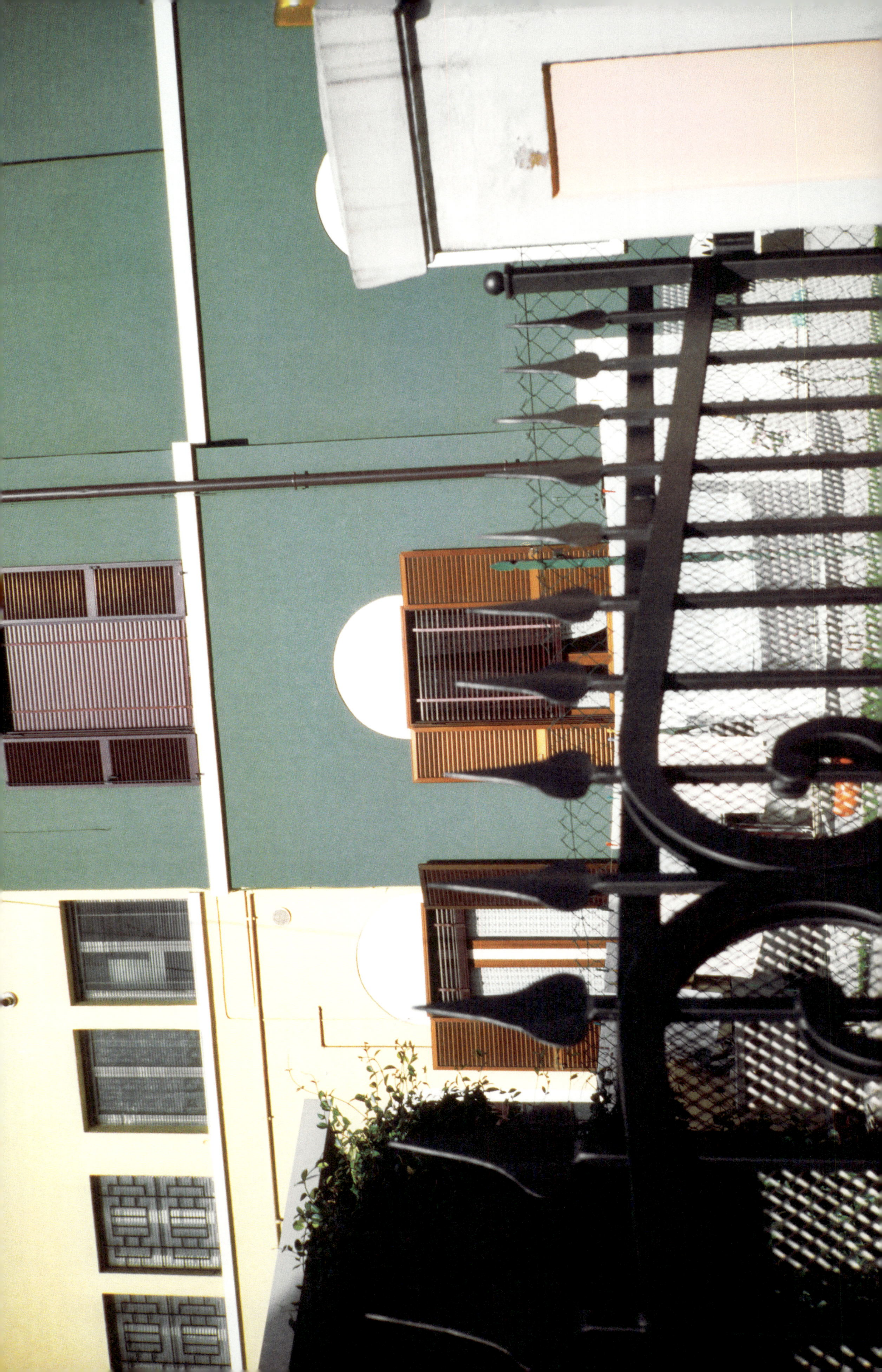

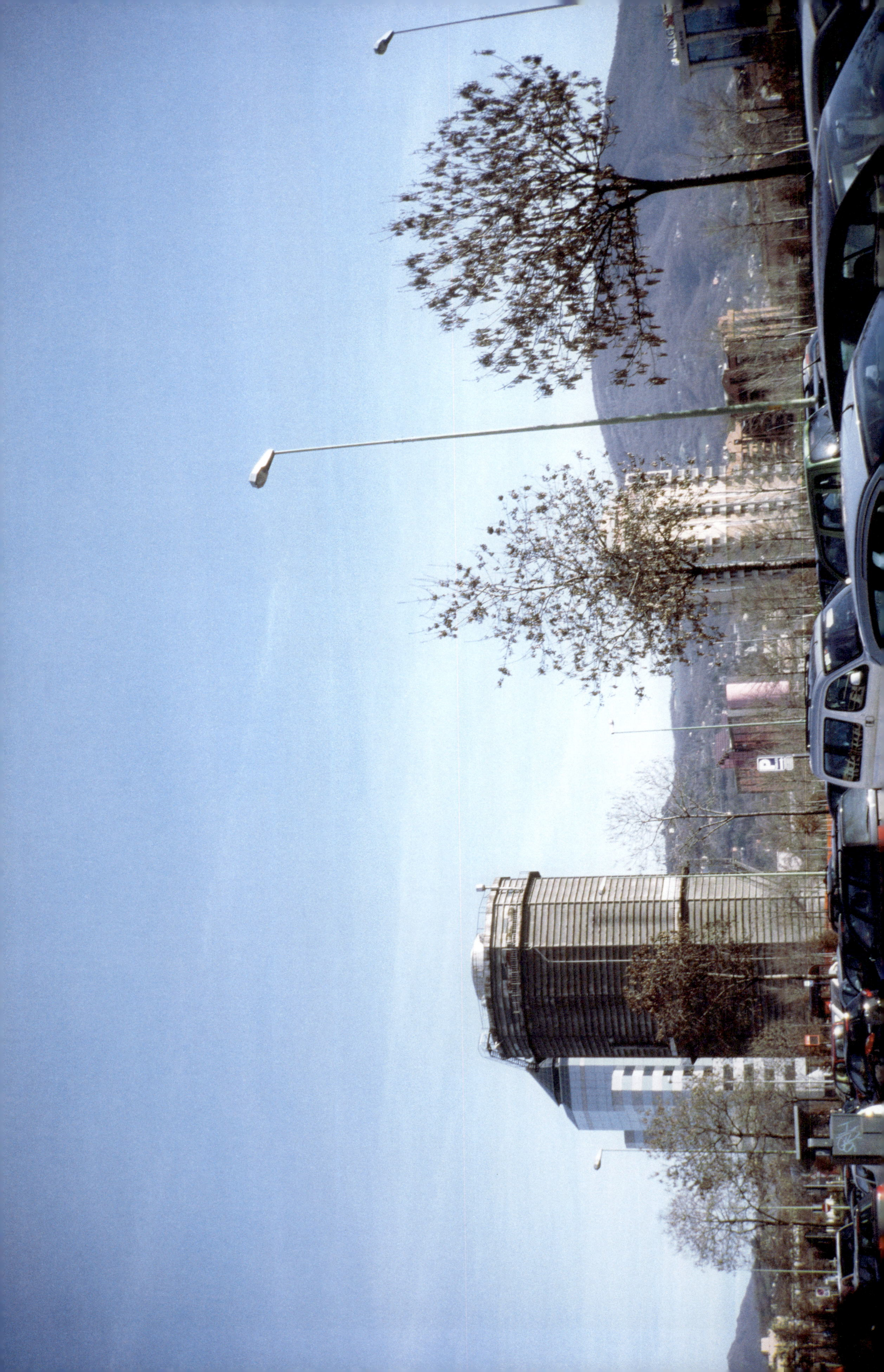

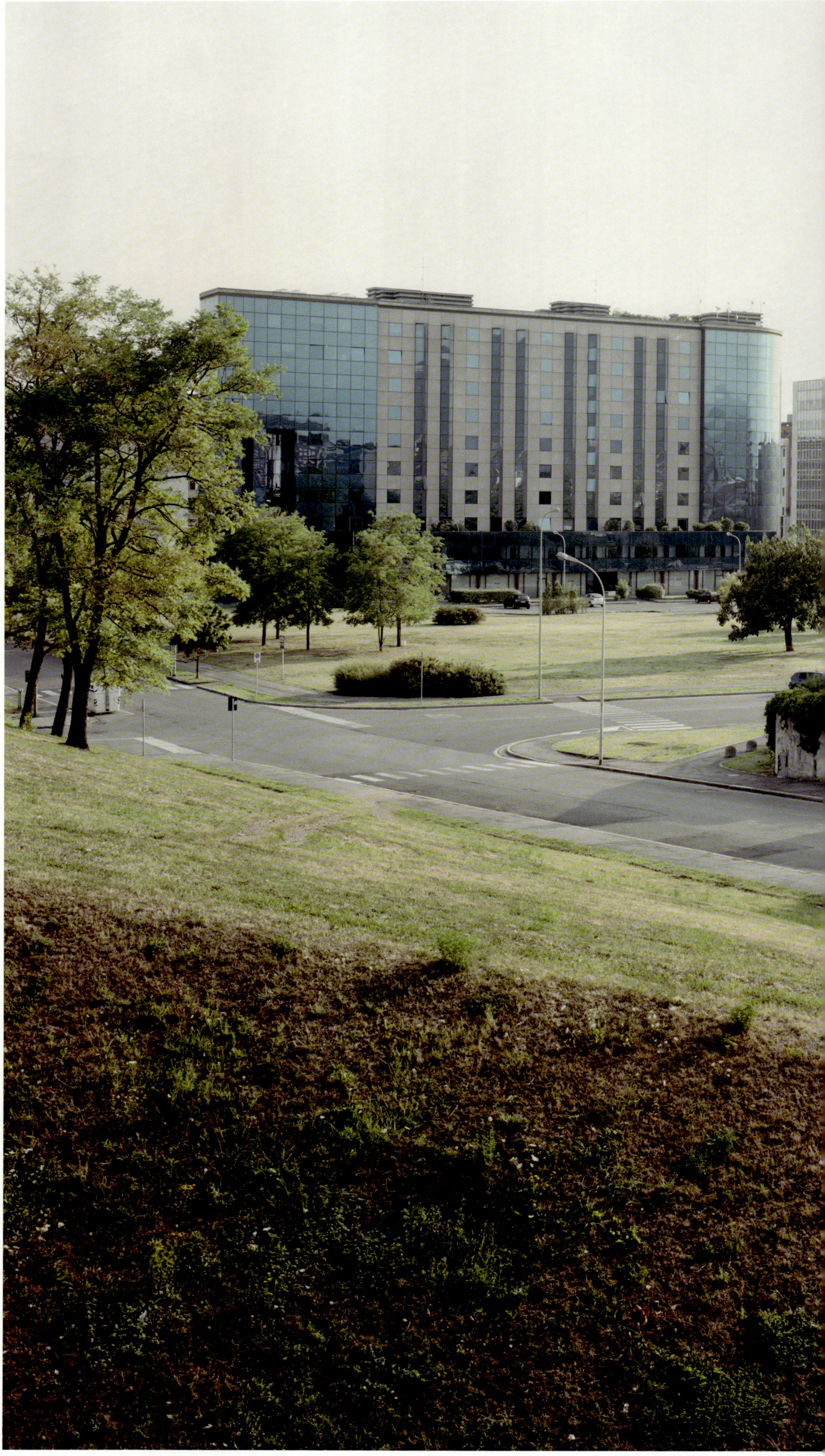

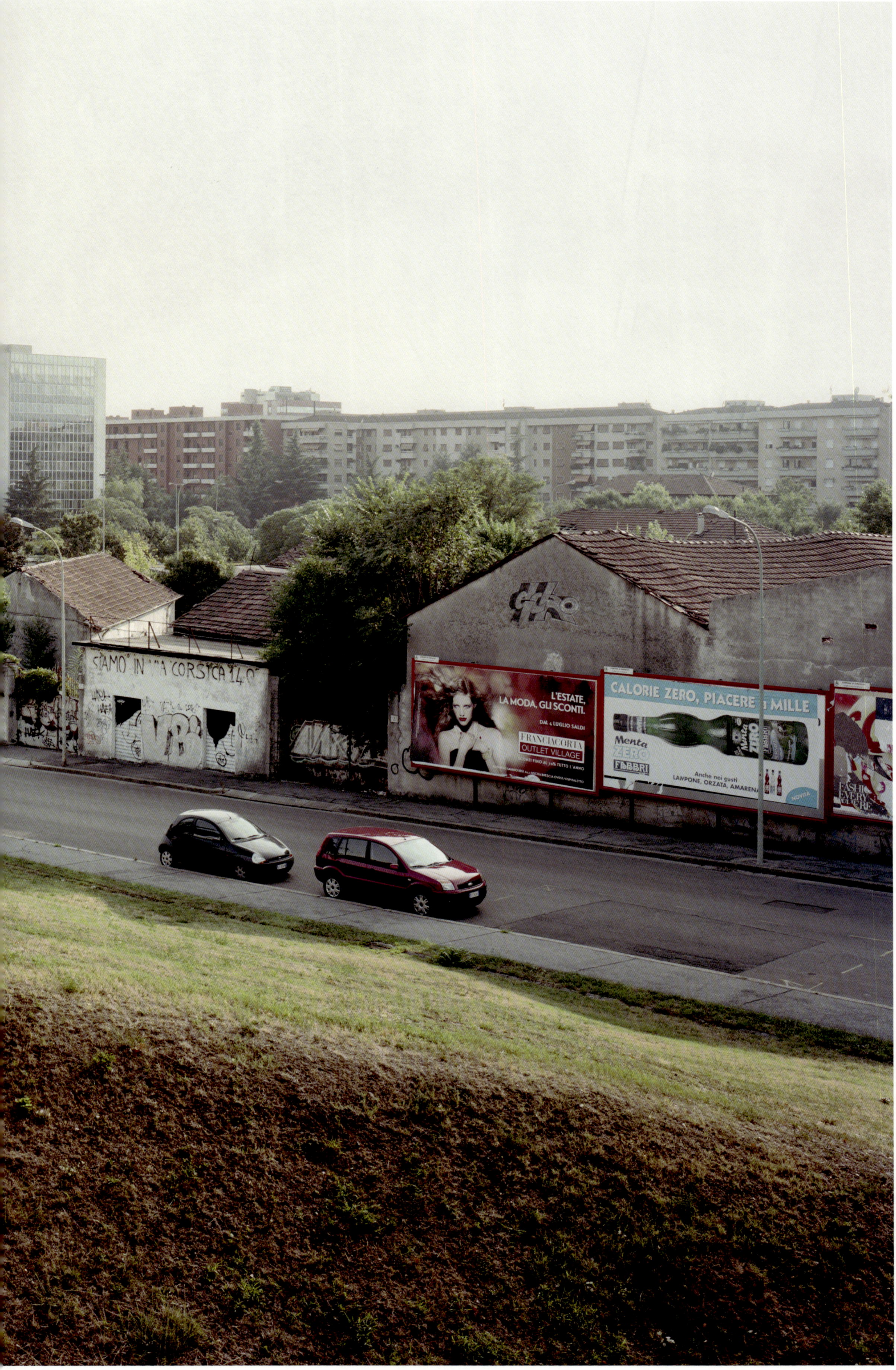
SIAMO IN VIA CORSICA 140
L'ESTATE, LA MODA, GLI SCONTI.
DAL 4 LUGLIO SALDI
FRANCIACORTA
OUTLET VILLAGE
CALORIE ZERO, PIACERE MILLE
Menta ZERO
FABBRI
Anche nei gusti LAMPONE, ORZATA, AMARENA
NOVITÀ

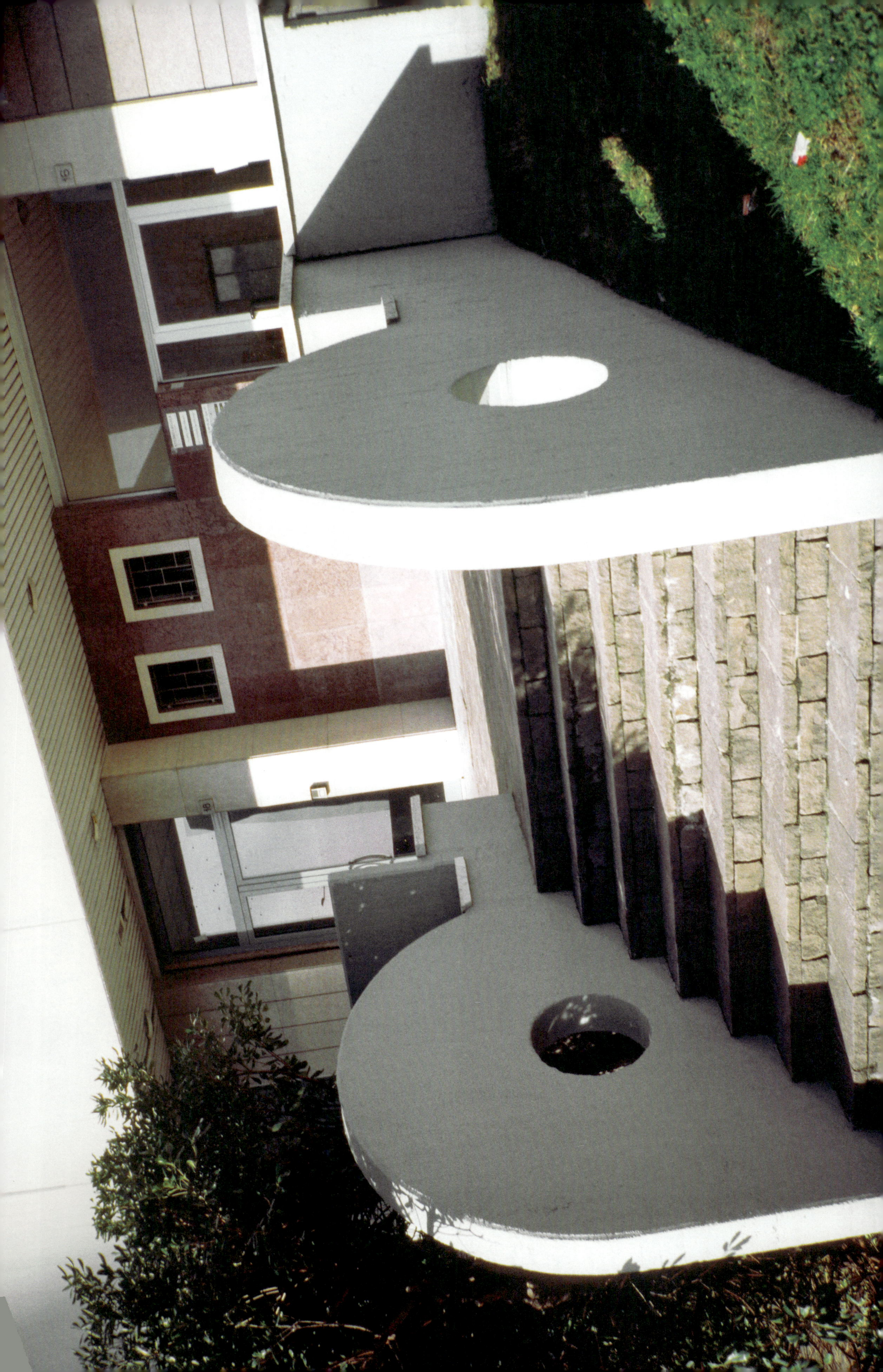

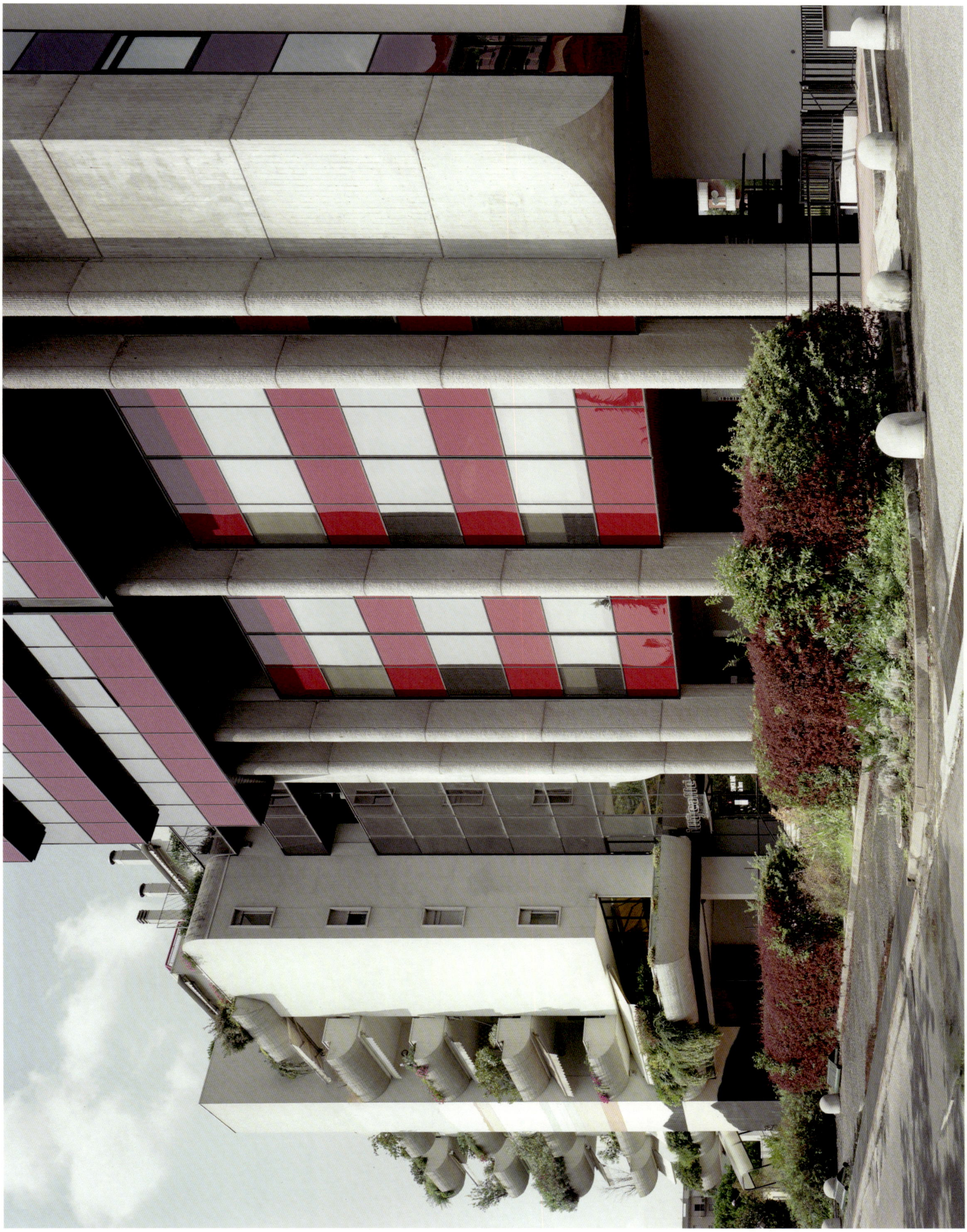

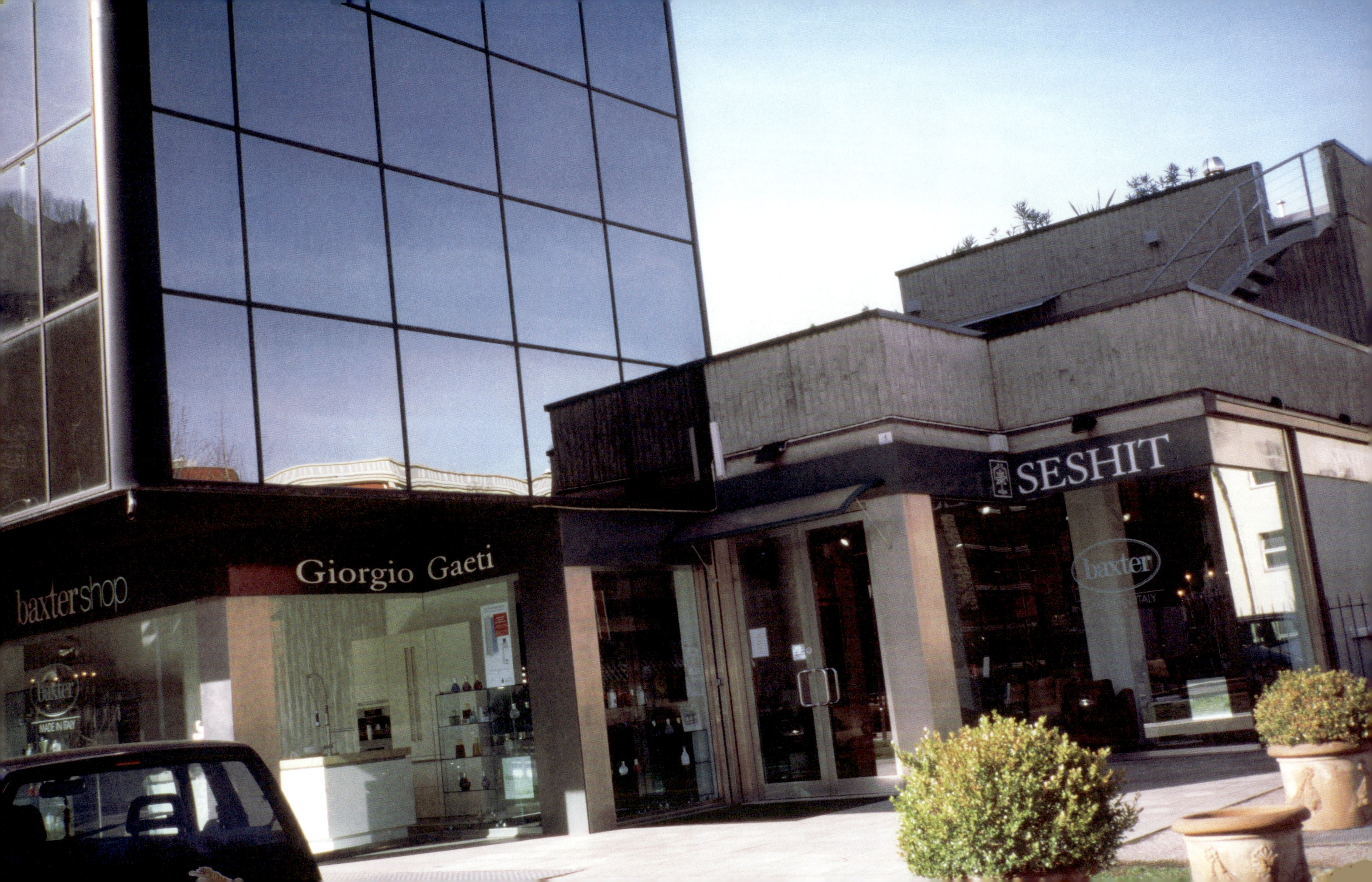

baxtershop
Giorgio Gaeti
SESHIT
baxter

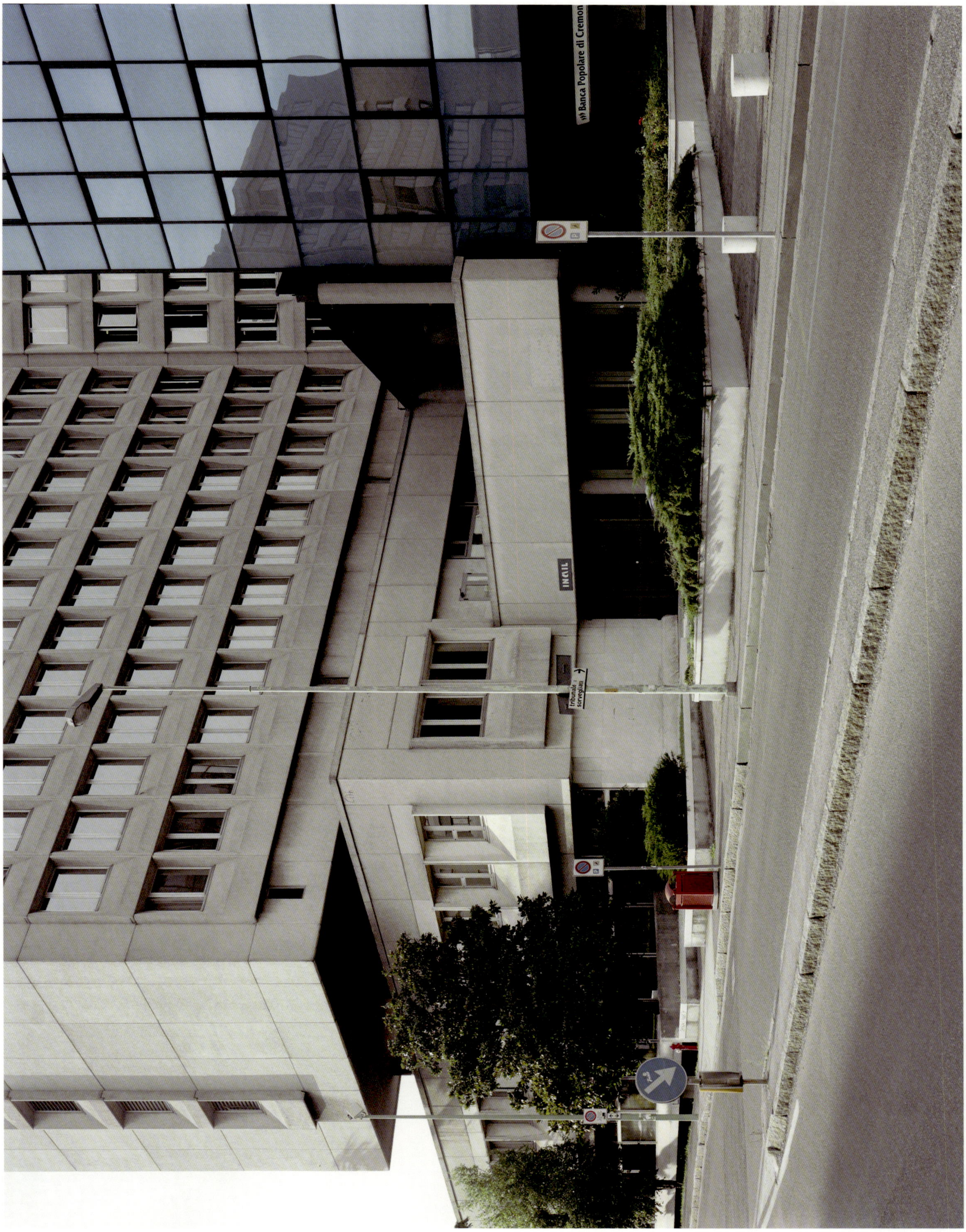
Banca Popolare di Cremon
INAIL

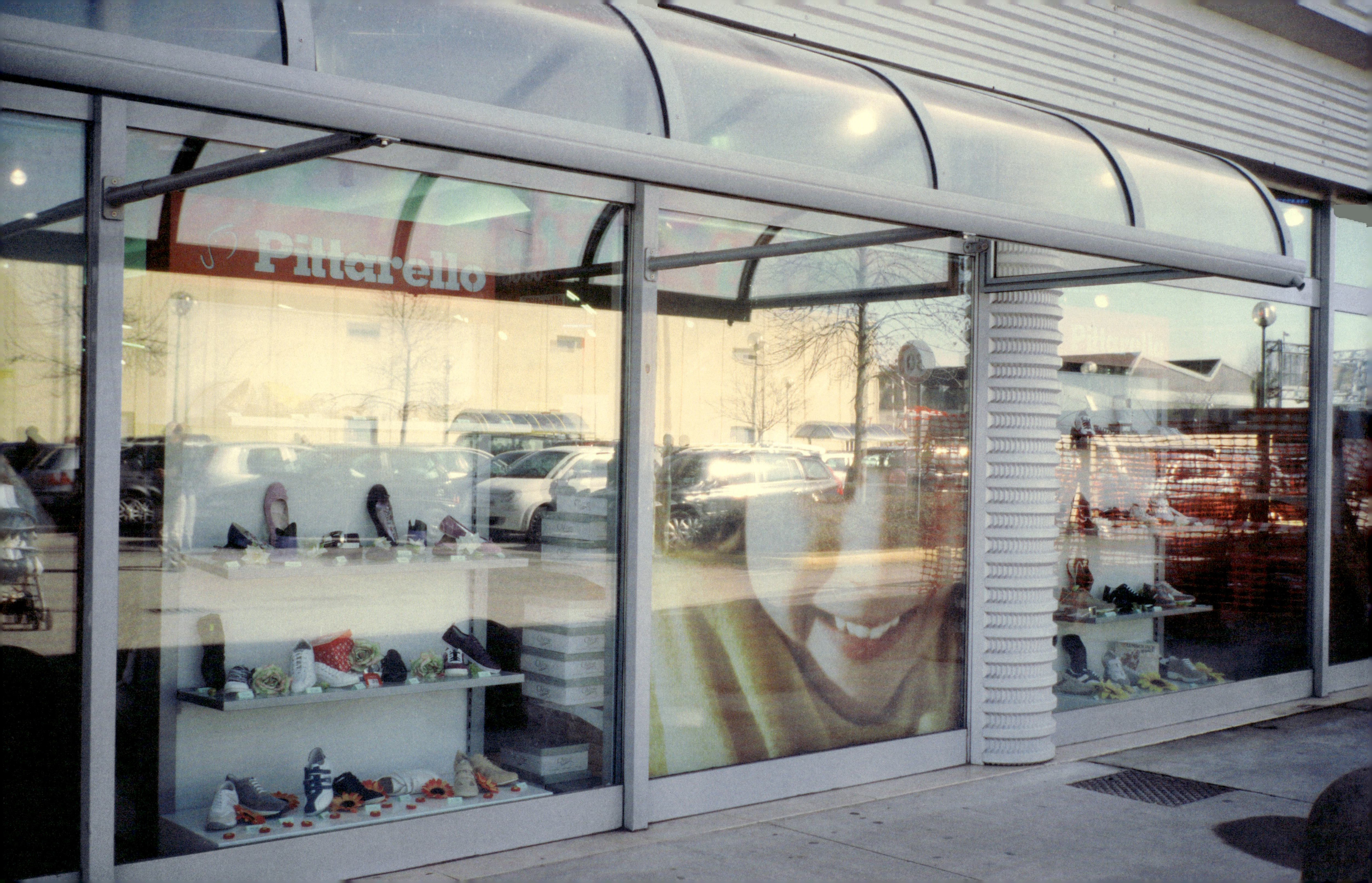
Pittarello

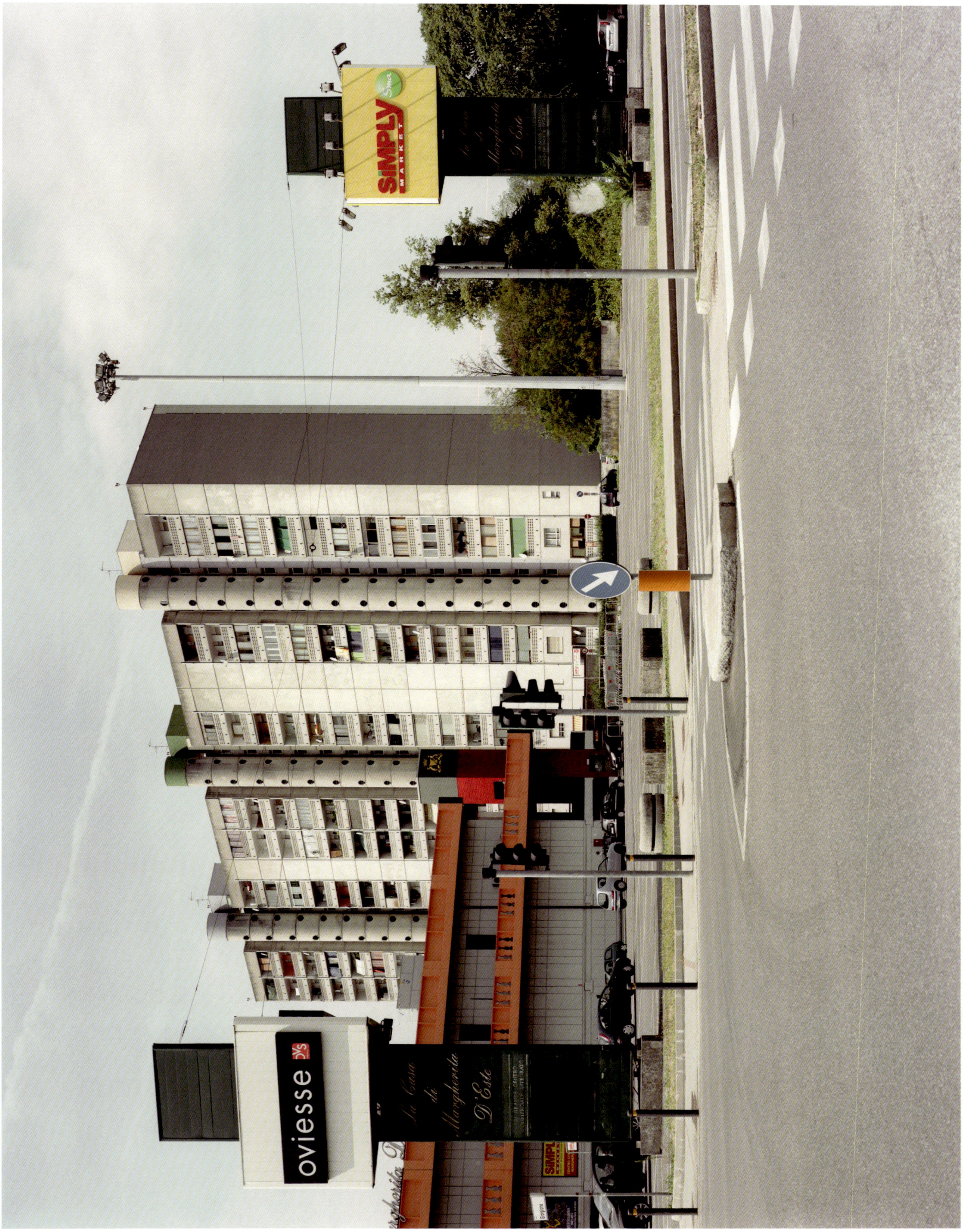
SIMPLY MARKET
oviesse
La Casa di Margherita D'Este

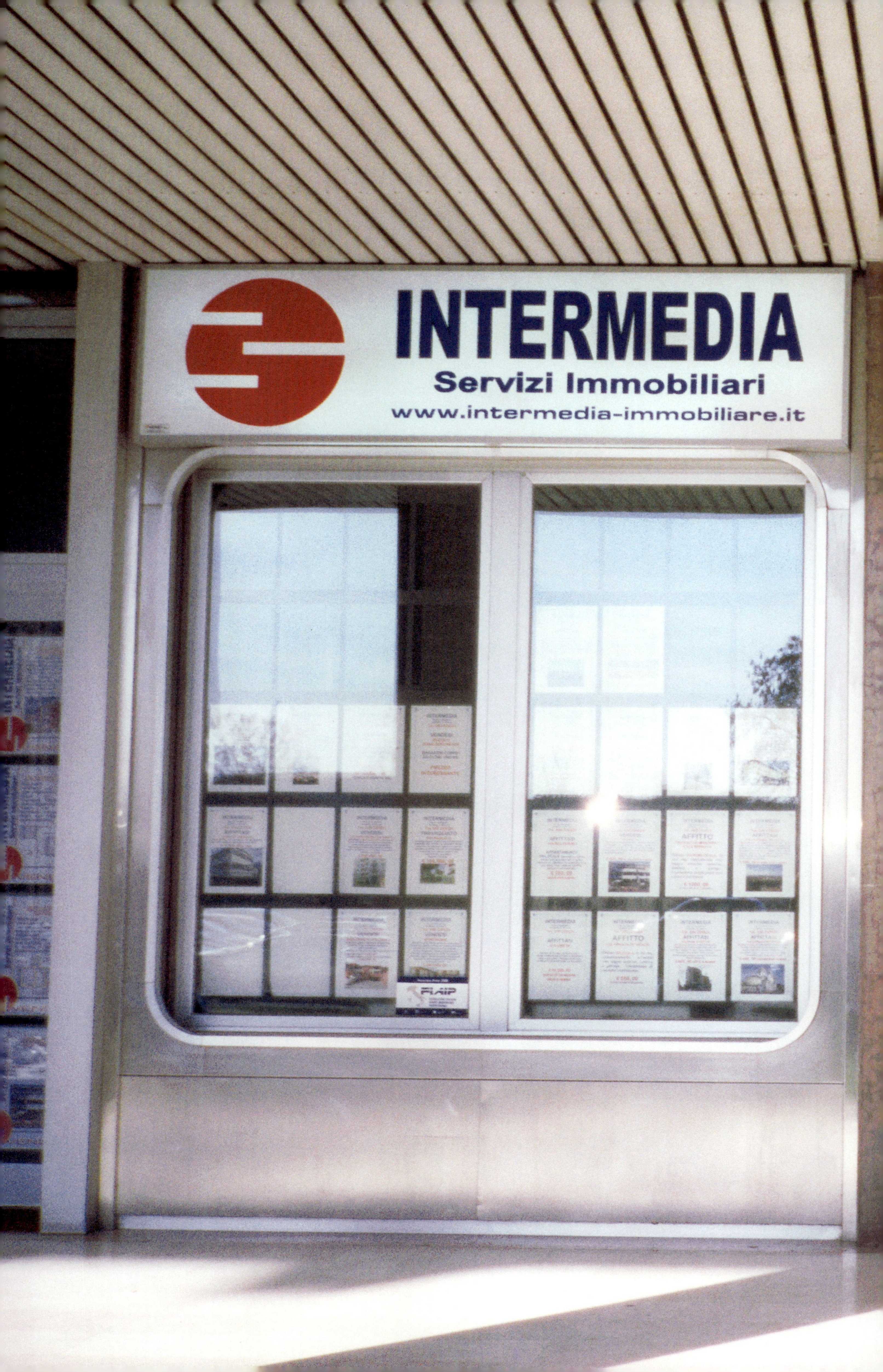
INTERMEDIA
Servizi Immobiliari
www.intermedia-immobiliare.it

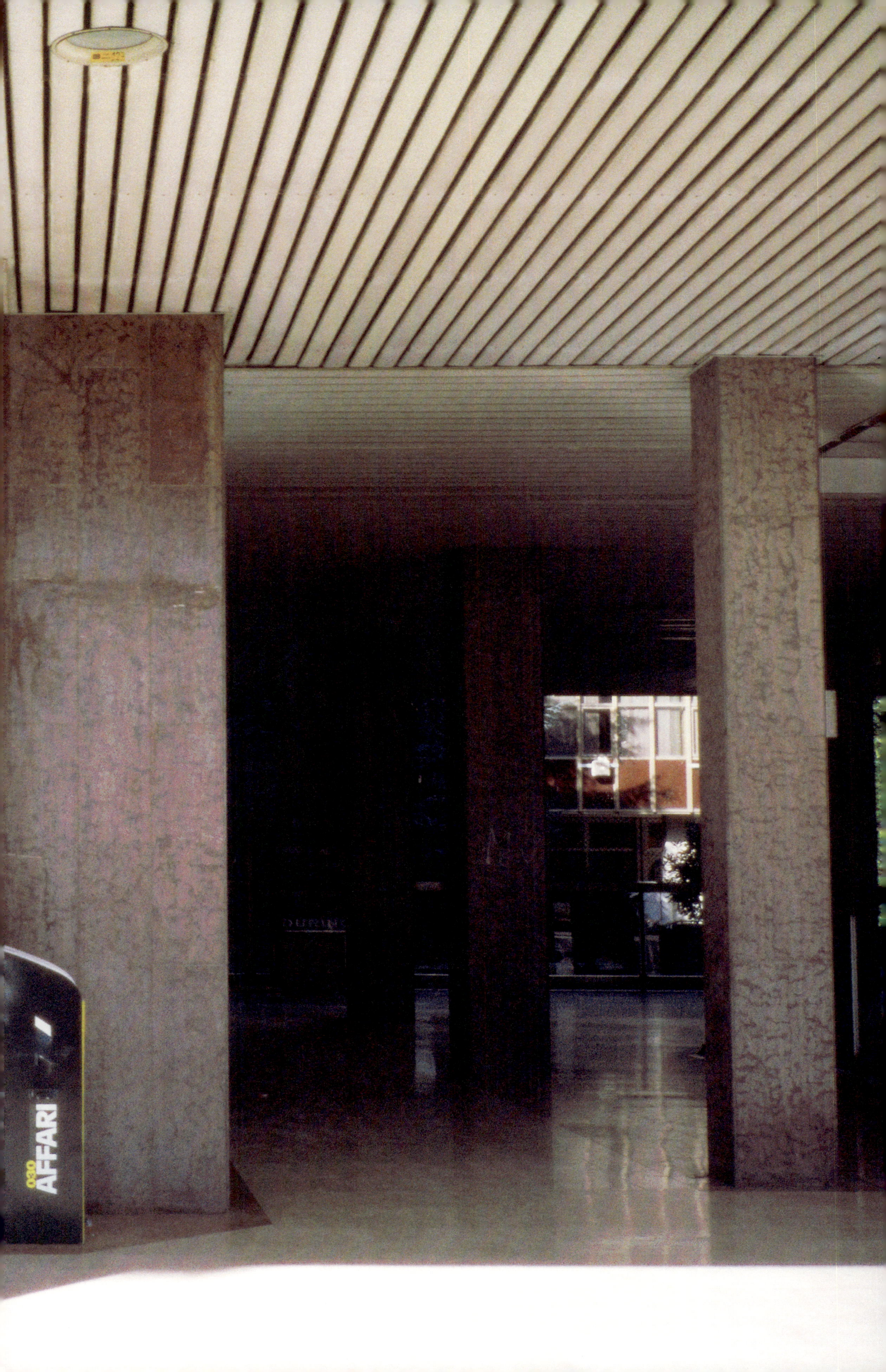
030
AFFARI

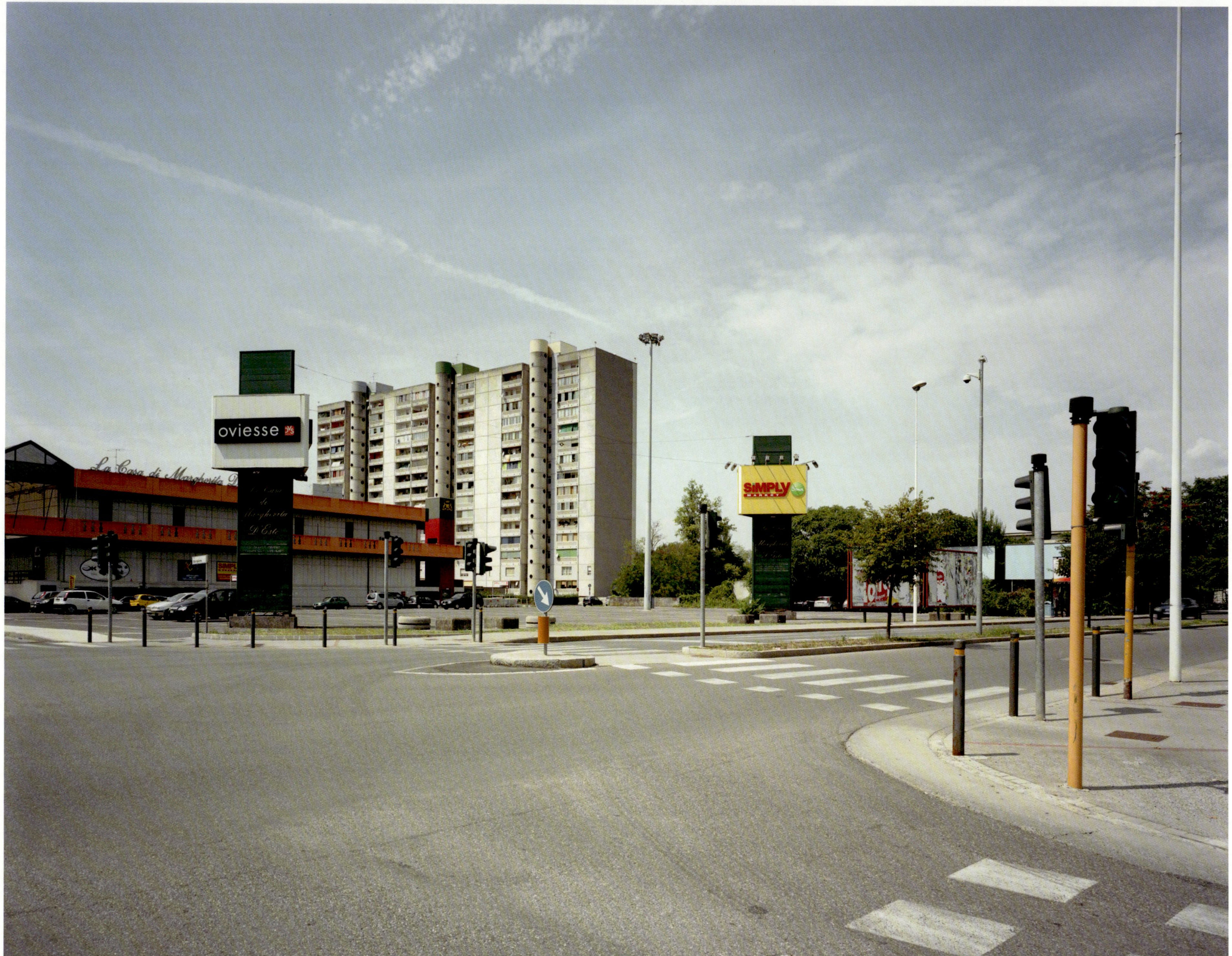
oviesse
SiMPLY

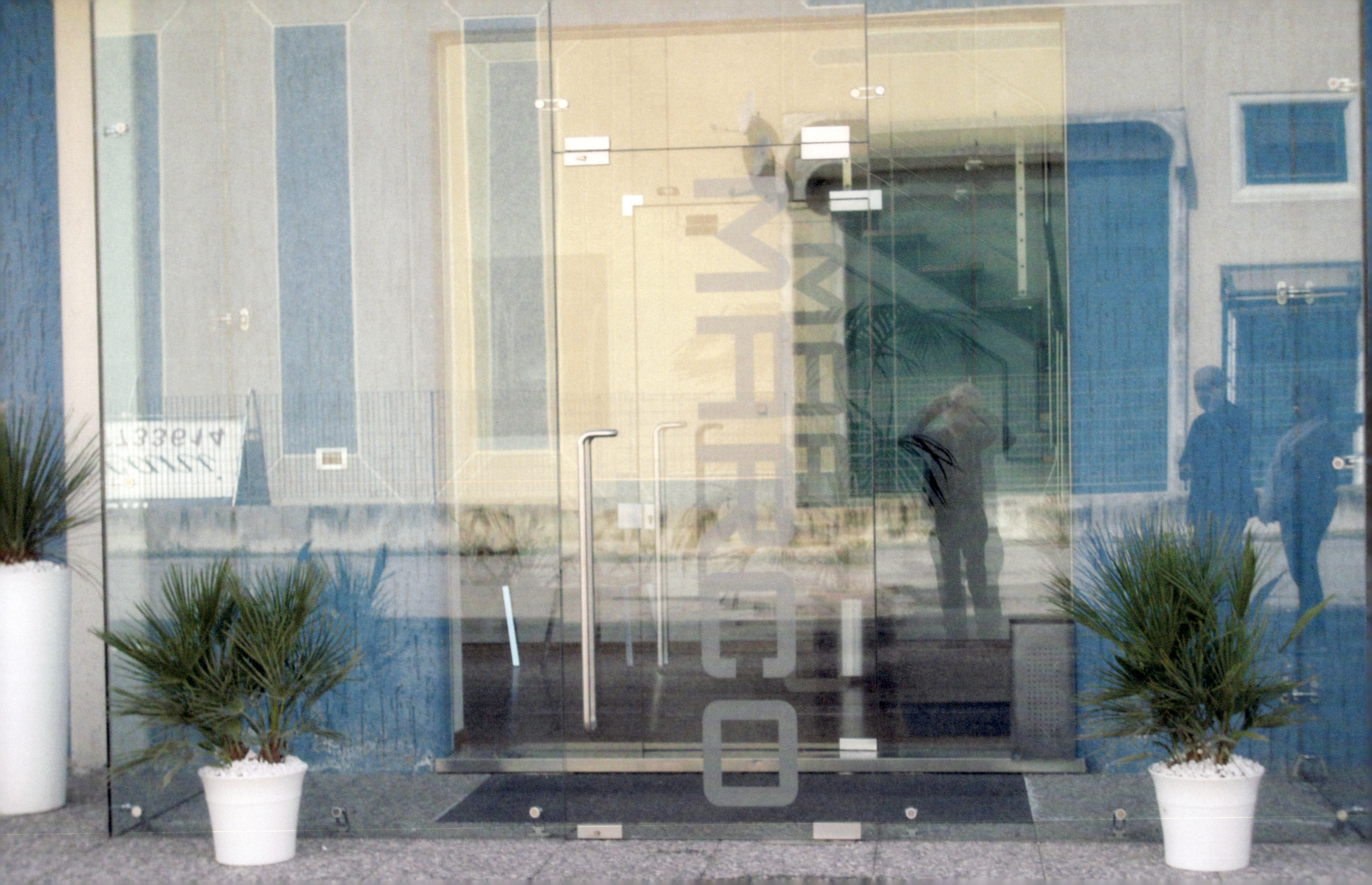
MARCO

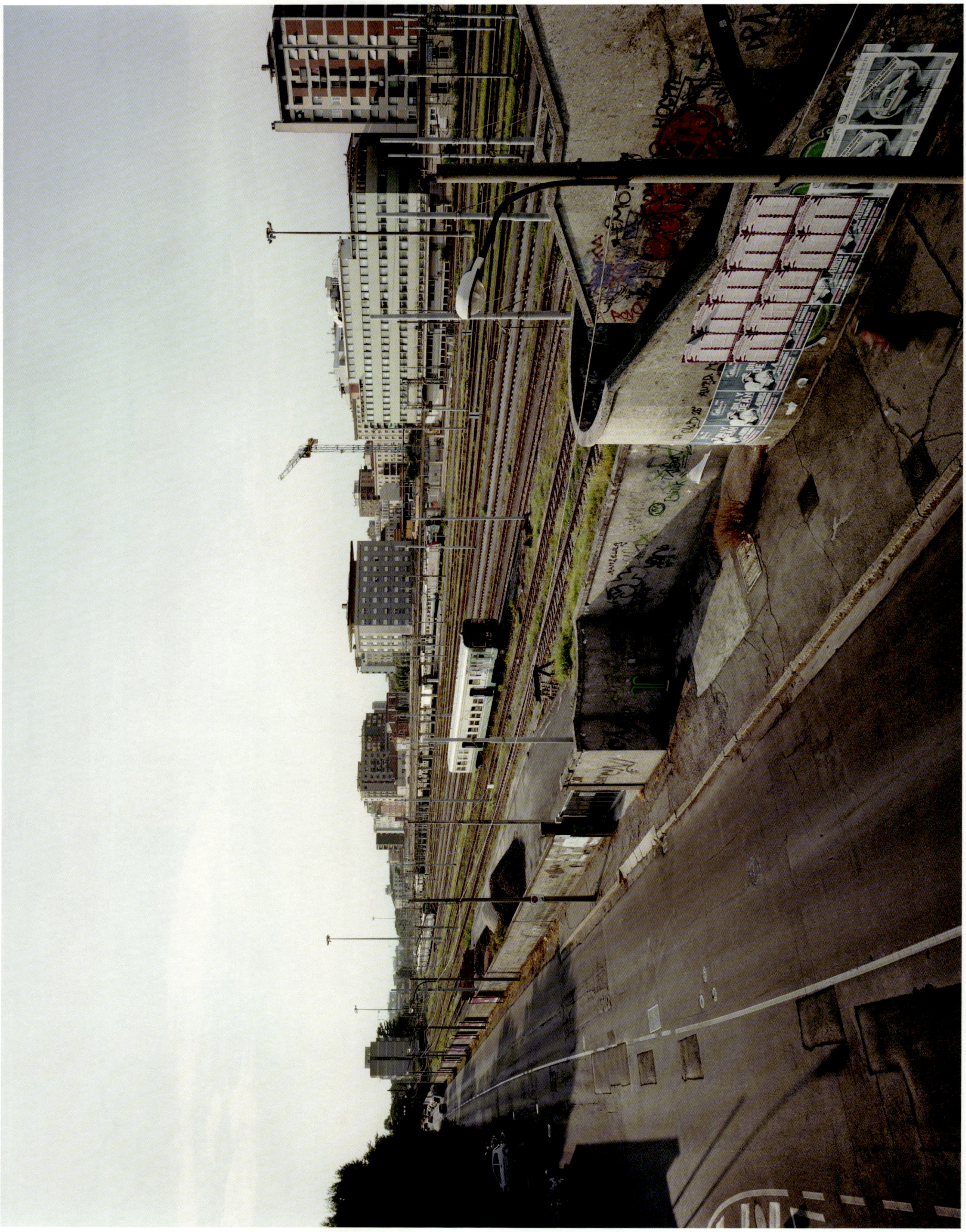

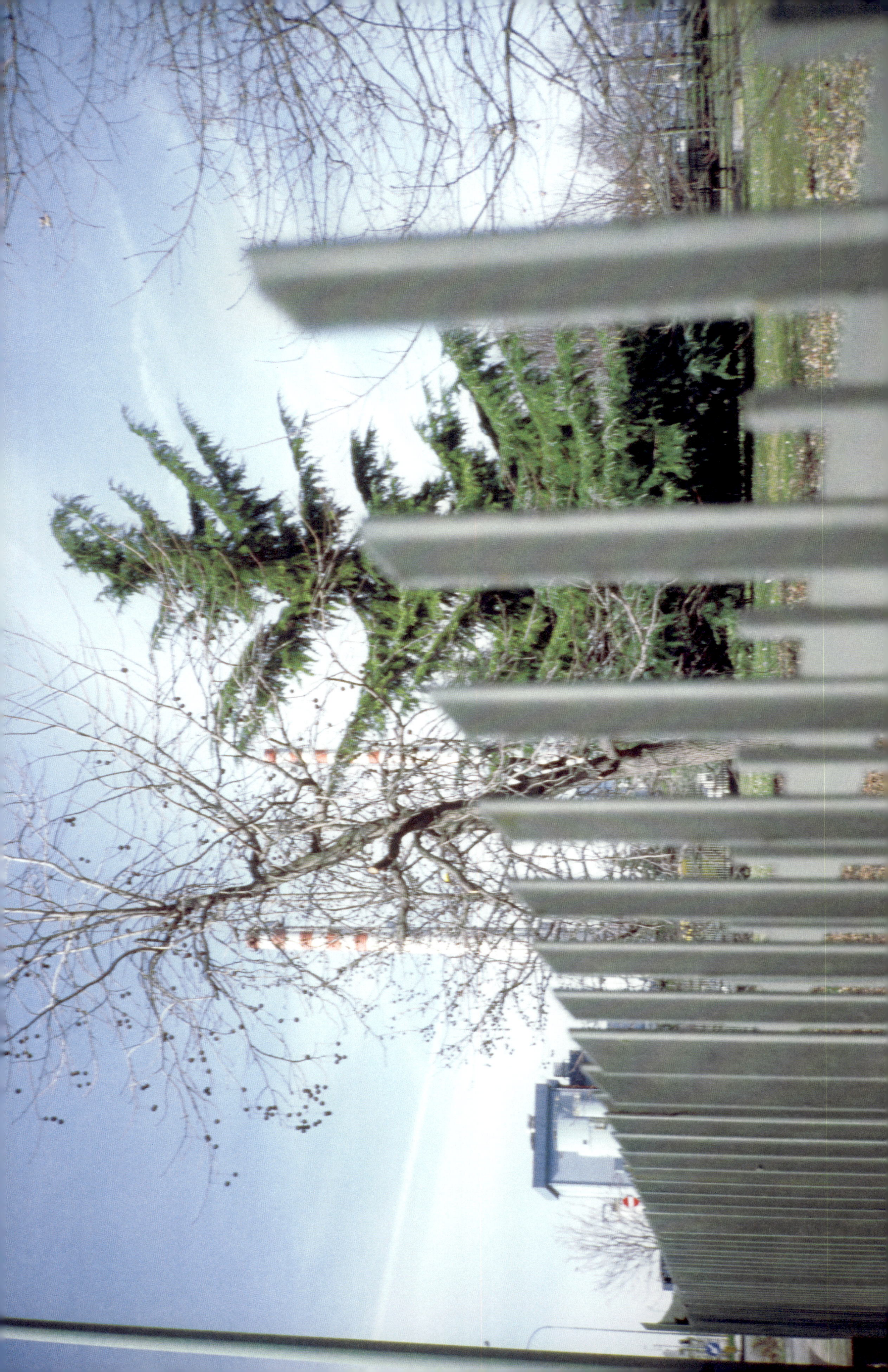

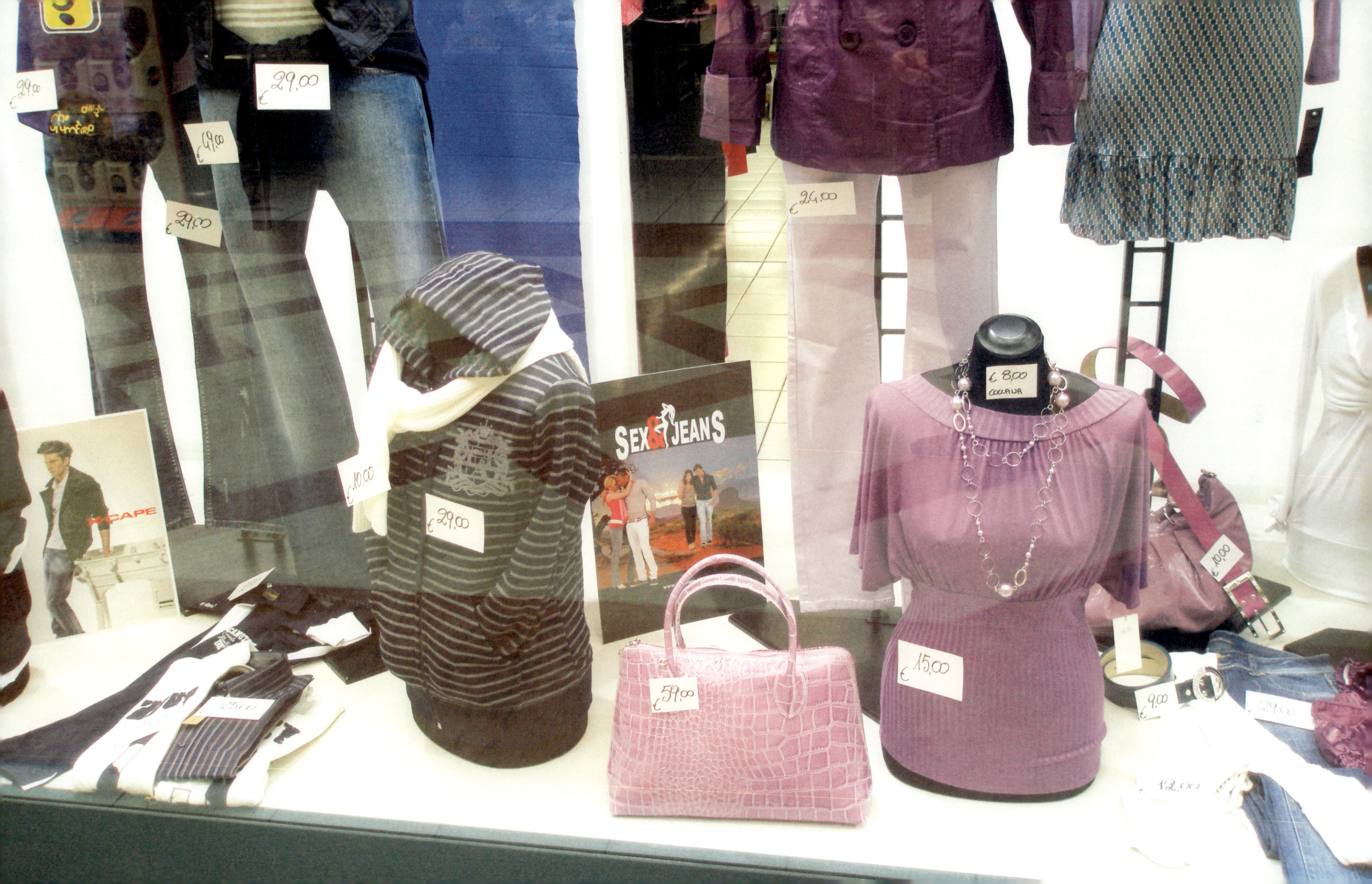
€ 29,00
€ 29,00
€ 19,00
€ 29,00
€ 24,00
€ 10,00
€ 29,00
SEX&JEANS
X-CAPE
€ 8,00
COLLANA
€ 59,00
€ 15,00
€ 10,00
€ 9,00
€ 29,00
12,00
25,00

Che cos'è una "Unidentified Modern City" (città moderna non identificata)? Come un UFO (Unidentified Flying Object), è qualcosa che noi immaginiamo essere il nostro presente/futuro, qualcosa nel quale noi viviamo, ma che ci saremmo aspettati essere completamente diverso da come l'avevamo progettato.

Le città moderne sono forse oggi il frutto del fallimento dell'utopia modernista, oppure sono semplicemente il prodotto di un processo di adattamento delle idee relative alla nostra vita futura, applicate alla contingenza dello sviluppo urbanistico che si adegua agli stili di vita contemporanea?

Da questa domanda è partito il progetto per questa mostra, che vede Gabriele Basilico, uno dei più importanti fotografi di architettura contemporanei, confrontarsi con Dan Graham, uno dei grandi artisti concettuali che ha investigato in profondità il rapporto tra pubblico e privato nella città odierna.

Il risultato sorprendente di questa indagine e di questo confronto è che l'architettura moderna, nella sua mancanza di identità, ha senso solo se è vista attraverso gli occhi delle persone che la abitano.

Il punto di confronto comune tra i due artisti è la scoperta di una nuova classe sociale che nelle architetture riflette i propri comportamenti e la propria identità.

Inaspettatamente, se dal punto di vista degli urbanisti la "Unidentified Modern City" rappresenta il risultato fallimentare dell'utopia modernista, quello dei due artisti è la focalizzazione di uno spazio urbano che indica un nuovo stile di vita sociale e la nascita di una nuova entità collettiva. In definitiva, l'affermarsi di una nuova positiva condizione di vita all'interno di un'architettura che ha perso il suo significato originario.

Se guardiamo attentamente le immagini riprese da Basilico e Graham ci rendiamo conto che, dietro l'apparente attenzione all'architettura – spesso senza la presenza dei suoi abitanti – si cela invece un grande interesse per le relazioni sociali che questo tipo di architettura ha ridefinito, dalle quali noi tutti siamo presi nella "città moderna non identificata".

La città campione per questa indagine è Brescia, città dell'Italia del nord di medie dimensioni, che i due artisti hanno indagato negli aspetti che le sono comuni a molte altre città sparse nel mondo con le stesse caratteristiche architettoniche e indipendentemente dalle dimensioni: Lione o Nizza in Francia, Manchester o Liverpool in Inghilterra, Francoforte in Germania, San Francisco negli Stati Uniti, Gwangju in Korea.

Il loro lavoro si è incrociato producendo un dialogo, una riflessione sullo spazio urbano di una città ritratta proprio nella sua parte più recente, che rivela nella sua apparente anomia l'identità di una classe media comune a molte città del mondo. I due sguardi offrono una doppia prospettiva che sovrapponendosi produce un terzo sguardo.

Basilico sembra osservare lo spazio della città creando relazioni tra un edificio e il resto dell'ambiente urbano al quale questo edificio appartiene. Graham focalizza invece dettagli, scampoli di città, come se il suo sguardo si identificasse con lo stato di flusso di chi la città è abituato a viverla dal suo interno.

L'edificio "Omnia Struttura" fotografato da Graham è una rappresentazione emblematica di un'architettura modulare e banale che viene replicata all'infinito nello spazio della città moderna, in Occidente come in Oriente, dall'Europa agli Stati Uniti, all'Asia. Ma questa possibilità di ripetizione contiene in germe l'identità di un nuovo stile di vita. Nella ripetitività dell'architettura si trova una nuova identità – o assenza di identità – che rappresenta uno stile comunitario nuovo, che è un gesto di liberazione da ogni identità sociale predefinita. È l'affermazione di uno stato sociale che è al di fuori delle possibilità di una vita progettata a tavolino.

Ritroviamo questa caratteristica in altri scatti di Dan Graham, come nel loggiato con il negozio che porta il logo Intermedia, nella pensilina con i carrelli del supermercato, nella lunga vetrina del negozio di calzature con all'interno la grande immagine pubblicitaria della teenager sorridente. Il volto sembra quello di uno degli abitanti di queste nuove aree urbane. La vetrina riflette le architetture circostanti e l'effetto è molto simile a quello del vetro semispecchiante che l'artista utilizza per i suoi padiglioni. In questa immagine il volto si confonde con l'ambiente urbano riflesso e il risultato è una perfetta rappresentazione dello spazio della "Unidentified Modern City".

Gabriele Basilico pone al centro delle proprie fotografie per lo più singoli edifici o porzioni di questi, ritratti con assoluta oggettività e precisione. Nel loro apparente isolamento, queste architetture richiamano continuamente il tessuto urbano circostante e, pur nell'assenza dei loro abitanti, queste aree parlano continuamente di loro.

La fotografia della Torre Tintoretto del quartiere San Polo, con le parabole alle finestre, i panni stesi e le casse dei condizionatori che punteggiano le strisce colorate che segnano i piani dell'edificio, diventa la rappresentazione dell'umanità che vi abita, anche se questa non si vede.

Gli edifici del quartiere Brescia 2, come quelli di San Polo, sono ripresi a volte da lontano ma quasi sempre collegati a una strada, che spesso occupa una buona parte dell'inquadratura. La strada, nelle immagini di Basilico, è tanto importante quanto il singolo edificio, perché funge da collegamento e consente alla città di essere abitata. Le strade sono la rappresentazione tangibile del fatto che le architetture fotografate dall'artista sono luoghi in cui si definiscono le relazioni sociali.

Il punto di incontro dei due artisti in questo progetto è la lettura positiva che entrambi danno della città contemporanea, che accomuna Brescia a molte altre città nel mondo. Entrambi lavorano su quell'aspetto che oggi definiamo "globalizzazione" e che ha rimodellato la concezione stessa di agglomerato urbano.

Per Dan Graham l'interno del McDonald's vicino alla Tangenziale Est è la rappresentazione di un ambiente che parla di una nuova umanità che vive felicemente dentro la città, senza memoria del passato.

Una delle sue immagini più significative è la vetrina dei vestiti di colore viola, con i prezzi ben in vista. Nella sua oggettività l'immagine descrive l'umanità che abita questi spazi urbani, la nuova middle class apparentemente anonima e senza tradizioni che rappresenta l'identità di tutti noi all'interno della città contemporanea.

Entrambi gli artisti descrivono la città negli aspetti che la rendono meno identificabile, ma allo stesso tempo vitale. Un'architettura che modella, e all'interno della quale si formano i rapporti tra le persone.

Gli edifici dal modernismo quasi onirico, individuati da Basilico, costituiscono le nuove possibilità offerte dalla città contemporanea, anche quando questa sembra contraddittoria e aver fallito l'attuazione della sua visione utopica.

Lo sguardo asciutto e oggettivo di Basilico sembra cogliere in alcune parti di Brescia 2 una rappresentazione marziana dell'architettura, in cui le persone si trovano a vivere in un presente che sembra un futuro improbabile.

Gli edifici da lui fotografati sono visti nella loro nudità di oggetti che non rappresentano un'ideologia, quella della città moderna, ma il semplice edificio in rapporto con il corpo della città. Non vi è alone di modernità nelle immagini di Basilico, ma solo ciò che i suoi abitanti vi vedono. Il suo sguardo di architetto che si è dedicato alla fotografia è quello di colui che è riuscito a spogliarsi di ogni preconcetto, per vedere l'architettura democraticamente, come la vedono i suoi abitanti. L'immagine della nuova sede del Banco di Brescia è un'immagine solare, positiva, ottimistica.

Vi è nel suo lavoro uno sguardo democratico che lo accomuna a Dan Graham. L'artista americano, infatti, è attento ai particolari che rappresentano il flusso della città e dei suoi abitanti, come si vede nelle sue immagini con le vetrine. La pensilina con i carrelli del supermercato è il luogo di riparo/riposo funzionale al recupero del carrello della spesa di persone che vivono una vita quotidiana, traendo ispirazione da quell'architettura oppure ispirandola. Tutto il lavoro di Dan Graham sulla città è finalizzato a mostrare le relazioni create dall'architettura.

La rappresentazione oggettiva di Gabriele Basilico e quella apparentemente casuale di Dan Graham della città, riunite in questa mostra, convivono all'interno di un doppio sguardo. L'uno attento a cogliere la vera natura del luogo indagato, l'altro a mostrarci lo spazio urbano come luogo interstiziale dove le relazioni umane si ridefiniscono.

Il doppio approccio produce una nuova visione sull'architettura dello spazio urbano contemporaneo della "Unidentified Modern City". La città contemporanea – nel caso specifico Brescia – con i suoi tratti di architettura banale, che i due artisti rileggono dalla parte di chi ci vive. Quello che emerge in questa ricerca sul campo è la condizione di democratizzazione che nasce da questo tipo di architettura non identificata, che Gabriele Basilico e Dan Graham, con modalità diverse, sanno mettere in luce.

—Maurizio Bortolotti

Dialogo

E' forse l'architettura il soggetto forte che permette tra di noi uno scambio e un confronto possibile?

Gabriele Basilico & Dan Graham

GB Caro Dan, innanzitutto ti voglio ringraziare per aver accettato l'invito della Galleria Minini a condividere con me un progetto di mostra nella galleria di Brescia curato da Maurizio Bortolotti. Siamo invitati anche a un dialogo scritto come testimonianza del nostro lavoro sulla città di Brescia, da pubblicarsi come testo nel catalogo.

Non è facile per me porti la prima domanda: tu nel mondo dell'arte sei universalmente riconosciuto come un artista che ha lavorato in modo concettuale su diversi temi, con progetti legati all'intersoggettività e alla relazione con lo spazio e con i luoghi, utilizzando linguaggi diversi, dal video, alla performance, all'installazione.

Io sono un fotografo di architetture e paesaggi urbani, e da oltre trent'anni insisto, con un'attitudine maniacale, a registrare lo spazio che mi interessa fotografare. A volte mi sento un po' come un collezionista di immagini di città che vuole completare la sua serie ma non riesce mai a smettere di fotografare.

E' forse l'architettura il soggetto forte che permette tra di noi uno scambio e un confronto possibile?

Io con il mio metodo ossessivamente ripetitivo, tu con l'attenzione speculativa, filosofica, e con lo sviluppo di un pensiero teorico che si rinnova nel tempo.

In tutta questa vicenda, che può occupare l'intera vita di un artista e di un uomo, si impone a un certo punto una figura che è stata determinante sia per la qualità del suo lavoro, che per la sua dimensione etica.

Parlo di Walker Evans, con la sua straordinaria capacità di descrivere e raccontare uomini e luoghi, con un'estetica rigorosa e sempre nel massimo rispetto.

Un uomo, direi, dallo sguardo retto, equo e raffinato nello stesso tempo.

C'è stata una mostra nel 1992, a Rotterdam, che metteva in relazione il tuo lavoro con quello di Walker Evans. Purtroppo non ho mai visto il catalogo e quindi non sono in grado di approfondire la questione, mi resta però il desiderio di chiederti in un modo semplice e diretto: quanto ha contato la personalità di Evans, e come ti sei messo in relazione nel tuo percorso di artista e di ricercatore.

DG Mi chiedi quale è il mio rapporto con Walker Evans.

Credo che ci sia una reale relazione tra l'uso di Aldo Rossi della poetica locale e l'uso di Venturi della poesia e dello spirito nel suo lavoro.

Anche se non ero influenzato direttamente dal suo lavoro, sento un'affinità in quanto il suo lavoro fa uso delle pagine delle riviste e questo rientra nel genere del fotogiornalismo.

Entrambi ci poniamo in rapporto con la serialità come nell'arte minimal e con le immagini cartellonistiche come nella pop art. Eravamo probabilmente affascinati dalla piccola borghesia ai limiti delle baraccopoli rurali industriali. In altre parole, ai margini dell'urbanesimo delle città.

Il tuo lavoro sembra riguardare la città italiana del dopoguerra in termini di nuovo piano urbanistico. Sei stato influenzato dal libro di Aldo Rossi dal titolo "L'Architettura della Città"?

GB Aldo Rossi è stato per me una figura fondamentale, come per tutta la cultura architettonica e per il dibattito che si è sviluppato in Italia e in Europa dopo il '68. L'ho conosciuto come docente quando frequentavo, da studente, la facoltà di architettura al Politecnico di Milano negli anni '60. Il libro "L'Architettura della Città" (1966), è stato, e penso sia ancora oggi, un testo fondamentale intorno al quale ha ruotato il dibattito sull'architettura. Il processo analitico di Aldo Rossi di confrontare i singoli edifici con il tessuto urbano, di dare profondità alla storia nel dialogo con il moderno, il rispetto e lo studio del "locus", sono, tra gli altri, alcuni dei punti di forza della sua instancabile ricerca. La nozione di "fatto urbano", il tema del rapporto con la storia della città e dei monumenti (teoria della permanenza), l'approfondimento insistente sulle tipologie, sono alcuni tra gli argomenti che hanno posto l'architettura in rapporto dialettico con la filosofia e con l'arte, e che hanno animato per decenni gli studiosi e le scuole di architettura. A proposito dell'identità dei luoghi, tema centrale per la ricerca della fotografia dagli anni '70, Aldo Rossi scriveva: "(...) Ogni luogo è certamente singolare proprio nella misura in cui possiede sterminate affinità o analogie con altri luoghi; anche il concetto di identità e quindi di straniero è relativo (...)". "(...) Ho sempre affermato che i luoghi sono più forti delle persone, la scena fissa è più forte della vicenda (...)". "(...) Credo che il luogo e il tempo siano la prima condizione dell'architettura e quindi la più difficile (...)". La fotografia, a partire dagli anni '80, in Italia e in Europa, impegnata come osservatorio del nuovo paesaggio urbano, è stata influenzata dall'arte americana e dalle discussioni teoriche che hanno segnato i decenni precedenti. Ricordo i testi di Robert Venturi "Complexity and Contradiction in Architecture" (1966), e "Learning from Las Vegas" (1972), testi importanti nelle discussioni aperte in ambito post moderno, non solo per l'architettura, ma il mondo dell'arte più in generale. A mia volta ti voglio chiedere: che influenza ha avuto nella tua vita il pensiero di Robert Venturi?

DG Il modo di pensare di Robert Venturi è stato molto importante per me. Egli ha davvero amato la stessa arte che abbiamo amato io, Ed Ruscha e Claes Oldenburg. La sua interpretazione della locale architettura della parte emergente della piccola borghesia suburbana è stata davvero importante per me. Credo che ci sia una reale relazione tra l'uso di Aldo Rossi della poetica locale e l'uso di Venturi della poesia e dello spirito nel suo lavoro. Il mio lavoro preferito di Venturi è quello nel suo museo per Benjamin Franklin per la Biennale Americana a Philadelphia. Ho incontrato Venturi ed è una persona molto gentile. In un'intervista che ho fatto con lui, ha menzionato che gli piacerebbe ritirarsi nel nord del New Jersey – nel sobborgo italiano della classe media che ha influenzato anche me. Il suo interesse è vedere l'orizzonte della vicina New York dal New Jersey. (Sua moglie Denise Scott Brown "Questo è un incubo, spero non accadrà mai").

GB Caro Dan, non ho mai avuto la fortuna di conoscere Robert Venturi, ma i suoi due saggi "Complexity and contradiction" e "Learning from Las Vegas" hanno avuto molta eco in Europa. Si può dire che siano stati una rivoluzione del pensiero, della critica del modernismo, facendo piazza pulita di quel timore reverenziale che è stato il credo ideologico di tante generazioni dopo il Bauhaus.

Venturi ci ha insegnato a guardare il mondo intorno a noi con occhi nuovi, disincantati, ad osservare ed accettare il paesaggio e la città con curiosità, con attenzione, mi viene da dire con sguardo democratico, mettendo finalmente sullo stesso piano l'architettura colta, quella firmata dai grandi architetti, e l'architettura ordinaria, banale, dove il linguaggio effimero, sovrastrutturale, della pubblicità si è integrato o ha sostituito, mascherandola, la produzione edilizia.

Questo approccio della visione e della critica, che alla fine con o senza retorica possiamo dire "democratico", è stato fondamentale per l'architettura e per l'arte. Anche la fotografia lo ha recepito in pieno, come nel caso dell'affascinante ricerca delle "Twentysix Gasoline Stations" di Ed Ruscha.

Le fotografie di Walker Evans sono l'espressione di uno sguardo etico, o come le ha definite il mio amico Luigi Ghirri, sono come delle carezze fatte al mondo.

Il mio lavoro ha come soggetto da circa trent'anni la città e il paesaggio urbano. Tutto è iniziato nel 1978 con un progetto sulla periferia industriale di Milano, che è la città in cui sono nato e vivo. C'erano già in quegli anni molti spazi dismessi accanto a fabbriche ancora attive. Mi avevano impressionato moltissimo le fotografie di Bernd e Hilla Becher "Anonyme Skulpture", il rigore frontale con cui venivano fotografate in bianconero le varie tipologie di archeologia industriale, la catalogazione, l'impostazione tassonomica del progetto, una ricerca maniacale, ossessiva, potenzialmente infinita.

Il lavoro sulla periferia della mia città, che è diventato qualche anno dopo una mostra e un libro dal titolo "Milano ritratti di fabbriche", non ha mai avuto però il rigore e la purezza di quello dei Becher, né forse il punto di vista equidistante di Ed Ruscha. E' un lavoro sullo spazio, sulla strada, sui luoghi, sicuramente influenzato dallo stile fotografico che dagli anni Trenta in poi, con la mission della Farm Security Administration, ha condizionato in modo inequivocabile il mondo della fotografia documentaria. E qui mi riferisco ancora una volta alla lezione del grande Walker Evans, con il suo sguardo comprensivo e rigoroso, estetico ma non compiacente, e alla sua definizione/nozione di "stile documentario".

Le fotografie di Walker Evans sono l'espressione di uno sguardo etico, o come le ha definite il mio amico Luigi Ghirri, sono come delle carezze fatte al mondo.

Parlando di questi percorsi e dell'influenza di questi importanti protagonisti della cultura e della ricerca artistica, è evidente che il campo, oggetto di indagini e di idee, è sempre lei, la città.

Capovolgendo il punto di vista, è la città stessa l'occasione per un confronto di teorie e di pensieri, distanti solo in apparenza, come quelli già citati di Robert Venturi e Aldo Rossi.

E' già stato osservato che nel recupero della città vernacolare, al di là delle ovvie differenze tra Europa e America, lo sguardo critico di Robert Venturi sottende un atteggiamento ironico, indispensabile per comprendere, fino in fondo e senza pregiudizi, l'identità del nuovo paesaggio urbano.

L'inventario delle forme che Aldo Rossi riscopre e rilancia come frammento per una ricomposizione della città, una "Collage City" rossiana, per dirla con Colin Rowe, non mi sembra contenere un sottinteso ironico,

Vedo un parallelo tra il lavoro di Rossi e quello di Venturi nel senso che entrambi trattano i ricordi d'infanzia del paesaggio architettonico della periferia locale in maniera poetica (e nel caso di Rossi secondo una varietà cinematografica).

ma al contrario fonda le sue radici nella storia, alla ricerca di un rigore geometrico e di un'essenzialità della forma architettonica.

Osservando le tue fotografie su Brescia, in particolare i soggetti che il tuo sguardo ha intercettato: vetrine, cartelli stradali, auto parcheggiate, porte, finestre, recinti, barriere, frammenti di un paesaggio urbano caotico e confuso, mi è stato quasi inevitabile pensare ad altre fotografie e ad altri fotografi e artisti. Mi sono venute in mente, per esempio, le immagini stradali di Lee Friedlander che ovviamente sono più costruite, più compiutamente "fotografiche", mentre le tue mi sembrano più documenti reali, apparentemente meno dipendenti dalla costruzione di uno stile. Sei d'accordo? E cosa mi puoi dire a questo proposito?

DG Il lavoro di Venturi non ha direttamente influenzato le mie prime fotografie delle case di periferia, delle fabbriche ai margini della strada, della segnaletica del New Jersey, ma dopo aver scoperto i suoi lavori d'architettura come la "Guild House" e la "Lieb House" sul lungomare del New Jersey, due dei miei primi modelli architettonici, "Alteration of a Suburban House" e "Video Projection Outside Home", furono una risposta al suo lavoro. Il lavoro di Venturi del periodo della "Lieb House" ha guardato al simbolismo della tipica decorazione ornamentale posta all'esterno delle ville indipendenti italo-americane, come nel caso della Madonna di plastica nella vasca degli uccelli posta vicino alla "Lieb House".

L'aver disposto un grosso videoproiettore sul prato davanti ad un'abitazione che mostrava tutto ciò che veniva trasmesso dalla televisione di casa, fu voluto per creare un emblema dello stile di vita della famiglia ai passanti che osservavano ai bordi della strada. Ciò si collega all'antenna TV color oro posta sul tetto della "Guild House" per le famiglie di quaccheri in pensione di Filadelfia, che aveva lo scopo di evidenziare l'abitudine dei residenti pensionati di guardare la televisione mentre rimanevano nelle loro stanze.

Venturi fu direttamente influenzato dalle fotografie di Ed Ruscha, così come dagli artisti pop come Claus Oldenburg. Vedo un parallelo tra il lavoro di Rossi e quello di Venturi nel senso che entrambi trattano i ricordi d'infanzia del paesaggio architettonico della periferia locale in maniera poetica (e nel caso di Rossi secondo una varietà cinematografica). Il "Cimitero di Modena" di Rossi mi ricorda l'interno di un centro commerciale di periferia. L'uso dell'ironia di Venturi è più caratterizzato dall'arguzia piuttosto che dall'essere caustico o critico. Infine, entrambi gli architetti sono attratti dalle case o dai rifugi di fortuna sul mare.

DIALOGUE:

ROBERT VENTURI, DENISE SCOTT BROWN, AND DAN GRAHAM

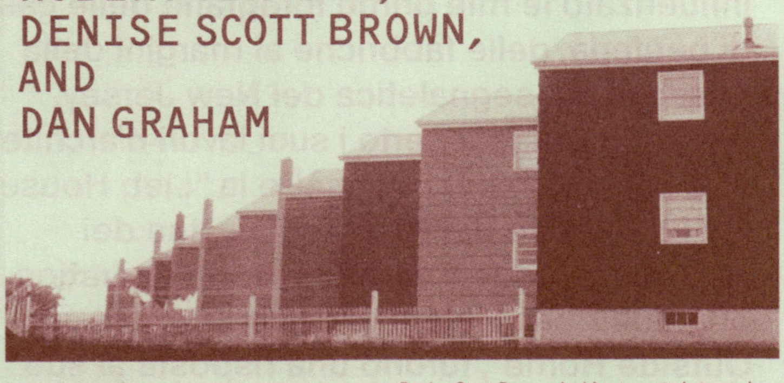

The artist Dan Graham's work has long been influenced by architecture, and his photographs of New Jersey capture an essential beauty of that state's vernacular landscape. (*Dan Graham's New Jersey* is up at Columbia University's Arthur Ross Architecture Gallery through March 23.) His love of both high and low architecture is shared by Robert Venturi and Denise Scott Brown, and Graham has written about the couple's American Pop Art approach in his essay "The City as Museum." *The Architect's Newspaper* went along to listen in on a conversation between the three in the offices of Venturi, Scott Brown and Associates in Manayunk, Pennsylvania.

Dan Graham: I want to talk about humor: I think your work is very funny, poetic, and humorous at the same time.

Denise Scott Brown: Architecture tends toward the monumental because of its size, and we use humor to tone that down. If you are a little self-deprecating, you take the wind out of your monumental sails.

Eero Saarinen also had a tremendous sense of humor, and you worked with him.

Robert Venturi: I don't see humor in his work.

I'm talking about the dormitory Hill College House (1960) at the University of Pennsylvania.

DSB: People say the alternating vertical and horizontal windows across the faces are like girls that nod and shake their heads. But I don't think that came from Saarinen. [When it opened, Hill College House was a women's dormitory.]

RV: I think the humor comes from other people. Saarinen merely meant his work to be an architectural expression; I've never been sympathetic to that idea. There [illegible] major conference organized on Saarinen [illegible] ars ago by Robert Ste[illegible] at Yale. He was f[illegible]ious because I am so ambivalent about Saarin[illegible] orked for him for 2½ y[illegible] the GM Tech C[illegible] 6–1955): Louis Kahn to[illegible] me [illegible] it, and I [illegible] oung at the time, and [illegible] di[illegible] d not lik[illegible] t. Louis Arch (1966) when it w[illegible] ilt, thoug[illegible] I do. I think architecture sh[illegible] uld connect w[illegible] conte[illegible] should [illegible] limited to one vo[illegible] y. Although each of [illegible] a different vocabulary, [illegible] 't particularly connect with place.

But Stiles and [illegible] lleges at Yale relate to th[illegible] le ki[illegible] hic o[illegible] pus.

RV: [illegible] that Gothic!

DSB: Yale Gothic [illegible] esting. It's smaller in scale and more suburb[illegible] n the Princeton Gothic and ha[illegible] y Arts and Crafts ele[illegible] t.

I l[illegible] [Dixwe[illegible]] fire station [illegible] 974) [illegible] New Haven, but un[illegible] y the firemen don't.

[illegible] firemen liked it well e[illegible] when we designed it, but 30 years lat[illegible] there are ne[illegible] firemen with diff[illegible] eeds, so they're changing it. [illegible] change [illegible] me, and [illegible] need to ch[illegible] heir buildings, but if th[illegible] ge is clumsy, some relation[illegible] ps will no longer make sen[illegible] ar[illegible] people blam[illegible] rchitect.

I l[illegible] linoleum flooring in th[illegible] station—[Josep Ll[illegible] s] Sert also use[illegible] n his ea[illegible] y buildings.

DS[illegible] love tha[illegible] We like [illegible] ese type of materials but we can't do it v[illegible] en, because some member of the client group says, "You can't us[illegible] um in m[illegible] ding." B[illegible] peopl[illegible] th[illegible] tation n[illegible] that the[illegible] ot g[illegible] consult with any architects and [illegible] ake the changes themselves. If yo[illegible] carefull[illegible] ed the rela tio[illegible] in a b[illegible] and som[illegible] changes the basic element…At the Seattle A[illegible] t Museum, th[illegible] cl[illegible] school entry [illegible] ay and t[illegible] d a congested l[illegible] y. They s[illegible] th[illegible] was the architect's [illegible] but it was because they changed the way the building was used. Change is understandable, but you should try to ask, "What was the intention here?"

RV: This is a problem with institutional buildings, which last a long while. When you design according to the needs of the original users, later administrators may change the program.

I once wrote an article on your architecture and mentioned Aldo Rossi for contrast, but now I think Rossi is also a vernacular architect.

RV: Yes, but I think he had a more literal connection with history than we did. Rossi's vernacular is Italian, and because Italian architecture has been a source for American architects, we interpret the Italian vernacular as historical—it's part of our history.

But since your work is American, it is immediate and present with historic echoes. This is the American way. Have you had any chance to see any new Japanese architecture? I love the work of Itsuko Hasagawa, for example.

RV: I do not keep up with current architecture because it generally does not interest me. I keep up with everyday architecture. But we have written about how we love the architecture of Japan and how much we have learned from and been inspired by it. We traveled there in the 1990s, but no longer have work there. I loved three things in Japan: the everyday of now—like the great eclectic mess of signage on the Ginza—and the historical architecture and gardens of Kyoto. Thirdly, I love the Buddhist architecture of Nikko. We still celebrate the first day we went to Japan as we celebrate the first day I went to Rome.

DSB: We knew about Japanese historical and modern architecture before we went there, but when we arrived, we discovered the urbanism from the 1950s and 1960s. It is exuberant, impolite, funny, and wonderful, and has a kind of naïve, semimodernist influence from American magazines, but done much better.

There are always signs is English!

RV: I love the signs!

Row of Tract Ho[illegible], [illegible] ayonne, NJ **(2006) is part of the show** ***[illegible] aham's New Jersey*** **[illegible] view at Columbia through March 23.**

Massimo Minini, Dan Graham, Gabriele Basilico.

MM Brescia è una piccola città come molte altre negli angoli del mondo. E' anche una bellissima città storica con importanti monumenti del passato, come molte altre in Italia, e un influente centro economico.

Ho chiesto a due artisti (uno fotografo, l'altro no) di avere un occhio per la mia città. Entrambi hanno ritratto Brescia ma in modi molto diversi: Basilico con un punto di vista professionale, Dan Graham con occhio distante, come un turista americano.

Abbiamo due opposte attitudini e risultati diversi.

Perché entrambi avete privilegiato i sobborghi invece della città monumentale? E perché Dan ha focalizzato la sua attenzione principalmente sui dettagli?

DG Caro Massimo, il centro delle mie fotografie sulla periferia suburbana di Brescia nel dopoguerra è stato definitivamente influenzato dalla mia esperienza dell'infanzia nella periferia suburbana di New York.
Il panorama della mia infanzia erano centri commerciali, Mc Donald's , industrie a bassa densità e piccoli uffici annessi agli edifici.

Brescia è una piccola città come molte negli angoli del mondo. E' anche una bellissima città storica con importanti monumenti del passato, come molte altre in Italia, e un influente centro economico.

Erano tutti collocati sulla nuova strada principale in espansione in periferia. Ho fotografato sia le case del New Jersey sia quelle di Brescia delle famiglie delle classi lavoratrici che, nelle loro nuove facciate architettoniche, si sono mosse verso la piccola borghesia (la classe sociale media), rappresentata nel falso "neoclassicismo" delle facciate con le connotazioni di falso lusso nei dettagli decorativi.

GB La cosa che mi interessa di più quando osservo una città è la sua trasformazione fisica recente. Mi interessa l'evoluzione del tessuto urbano, e questo è avvenuto fino a ieri, spesso nelle aree esterne di una città, nelle periferie. Anch'io sono sensibile alle grandi opere di architettura, sia storiche che contemporanee, ma penso che la città sia tutto questo insieme, architettura ed edilizia banale, la convivenza di luoghi diversi che spesso si risolve in disordine e anarchia ed è proprio lì che lo sguardo del fotografo può indagare, cercare di ricomporre nel caos armonia ed equilibrio.

Le parole di Alvaro Siza, scritte per la prefazione del mio libro "Cityscapes" (1999) descrivono come si può guardare un fenomeno urbano con occhi diversi: "Arrivò in Portogallo, una ventina di anni fa, un architetto brasiliano, Carlos Nelson, che stava dirigendo la ricostruzione di una favela di Rio de Janeiro. Presentò il suo progetto proiettando diapositive che mostravano i lavori in corso. Una colorata mescolanza di lotta urbana, "autocostruzione", samba e poesia. Desiderava scrivere un libro e aveva già il titolo: "Dalla favela alla città". Mi commosse l'idea di una città rinnovata, ma non sappiamo quale, che sarebbe sorta dalla periferia, dalle bidonvilles, dalle favelas più che dalla memoria dei centri storici".

A Brescia ho scelto la zona a sud della città, oltre l'autostrada e la ferrovia, quella che si sviluppa similmente a una new town, una città terziaria che può accogliere qualche mini-grattacielo, alcuni condomini a schiera, un lungo rettangolo di verde (futuro parco

Il panorama della mia infanzia erano centri commerciali, Mc Donald's, industrie a bassa densità e piccoli uffici annessi agli edifici.

attrezzato?), con uno stile architettonico che oscilla tra postmoderno e neomodernismo. Mi è piaciuto accompagnare le immagini che raccontano questa espansione urbana recentissima con altre fotografie dedicate ad un quartiere di edilizia popolare sorto a sud est di Brescia negli anni '70: sequenza di case a schiera parallele a comporre un sistema, connesse tra di loro da passerelle di scorrimento che si staccano da terra per marcare, quali improbabili porte urbane, gli accessi alle lunghe stecche residenziali. Infine edifici alti, compatti, snelli, colorati, traforati da centinaia di finestre, che si innalzano in modo perpendicolare nella trama delle stecche orizzontali, quasi land mark, visibili a distanza nel territorio. Qualche fotografia dedicata a Piazza della Vittoria, lo sventramento con la ricostruzione monumentale realizzati nel centro della città, vuole simbolicamente significare il primo intervento urbano in epoca moderna, compiuto durante gli anni del regime.

Index

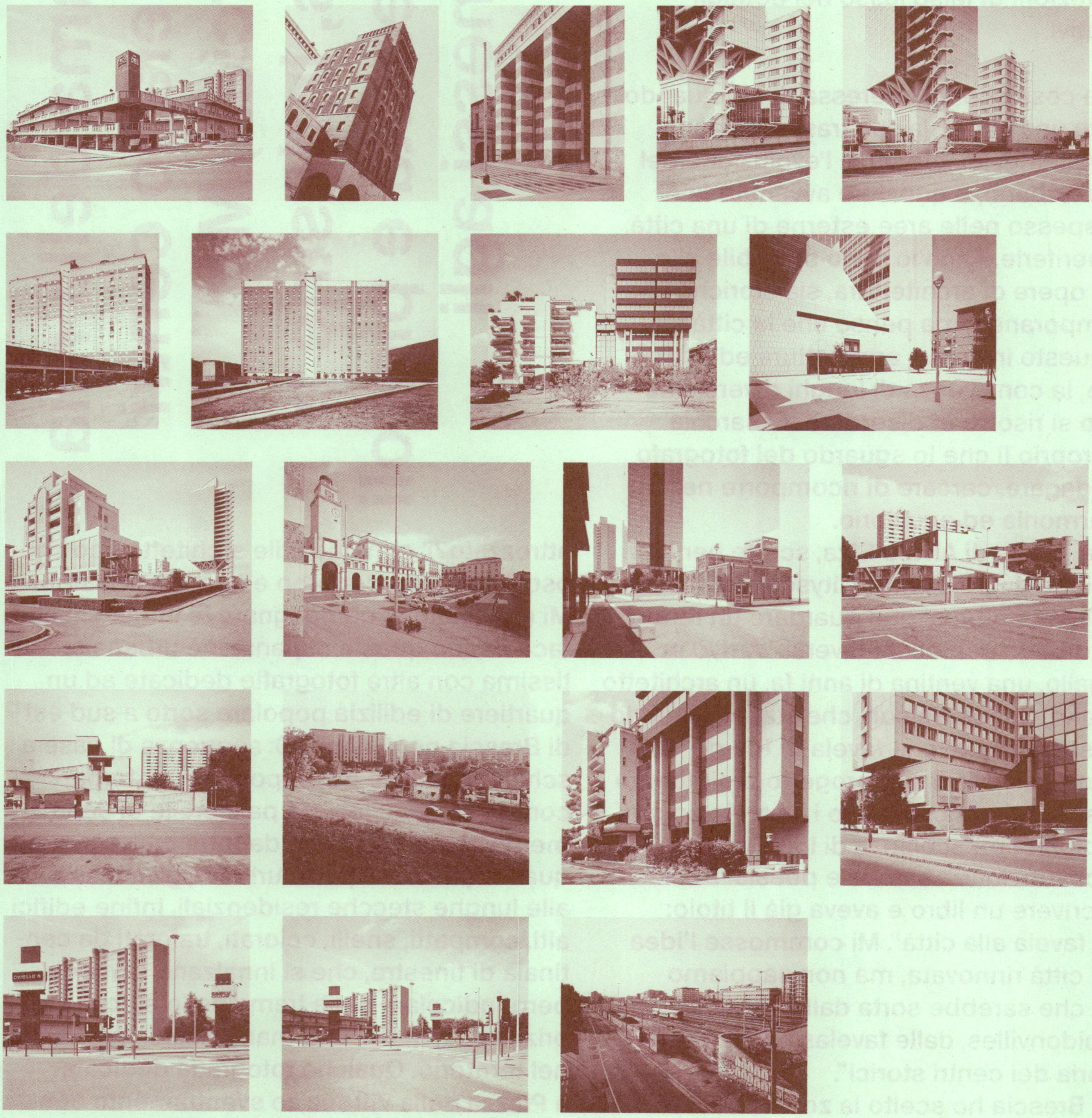

Gabriele Basilico

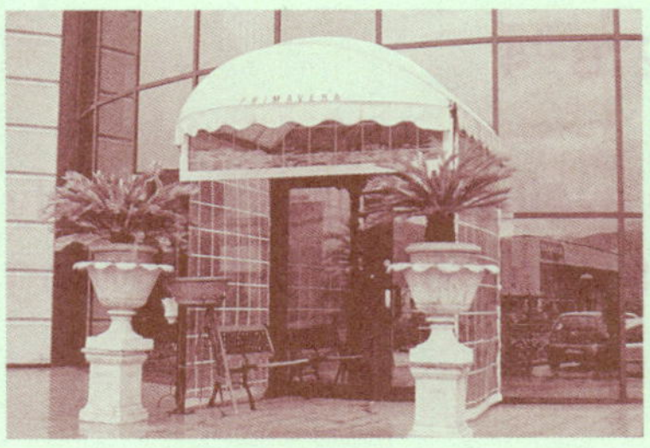
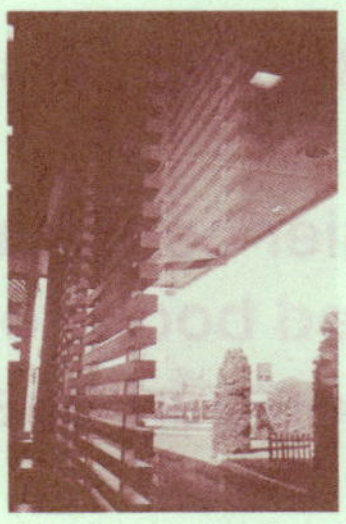
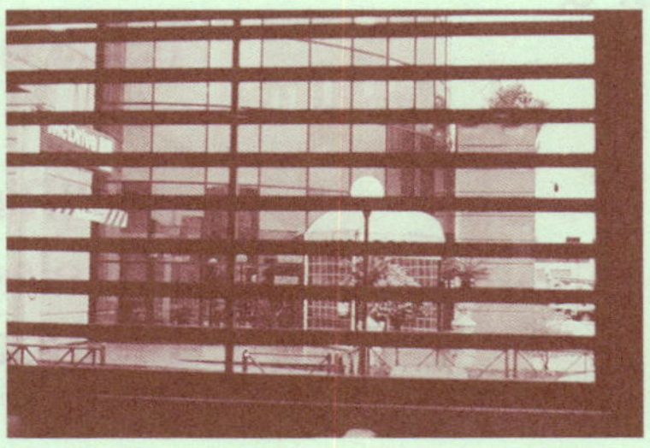
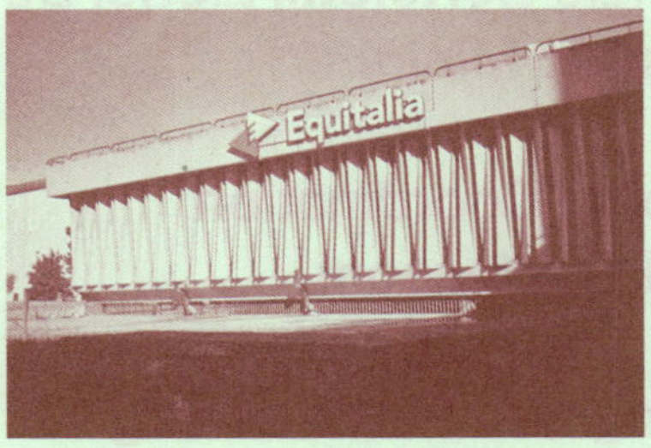

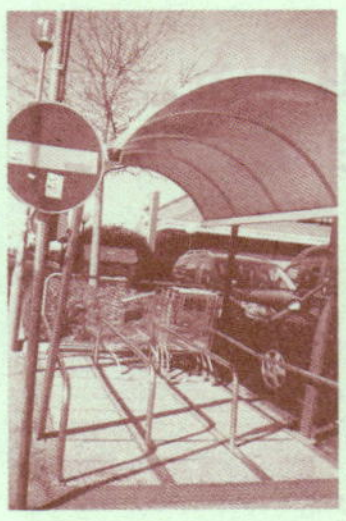
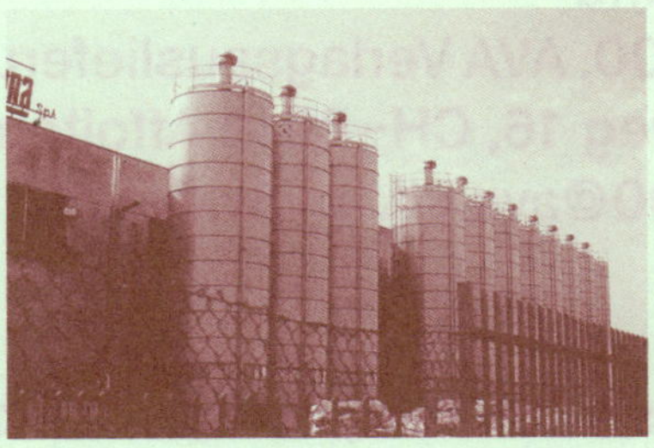
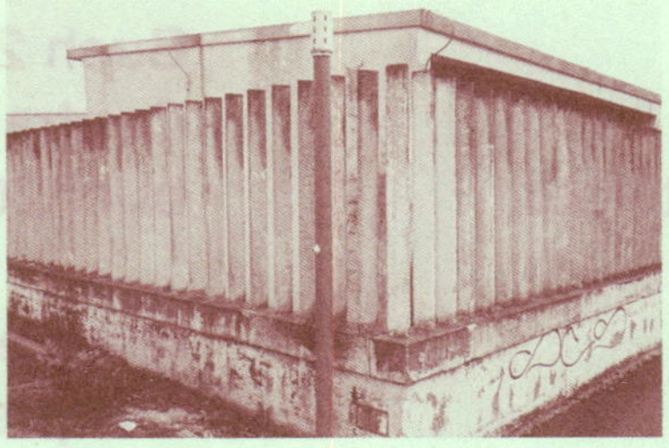
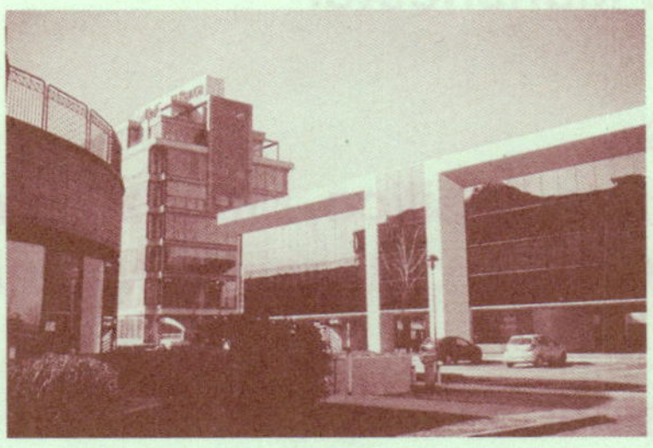
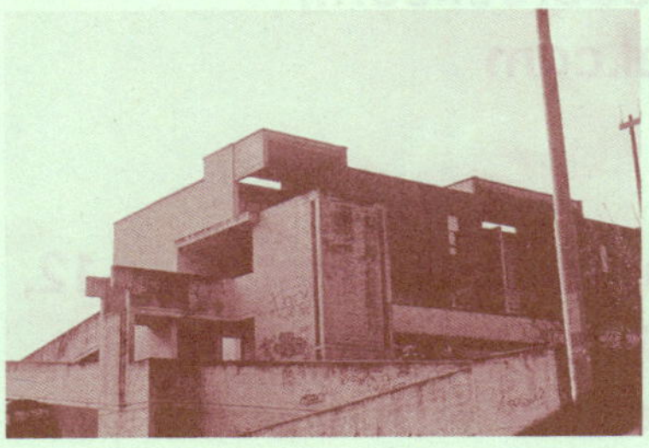
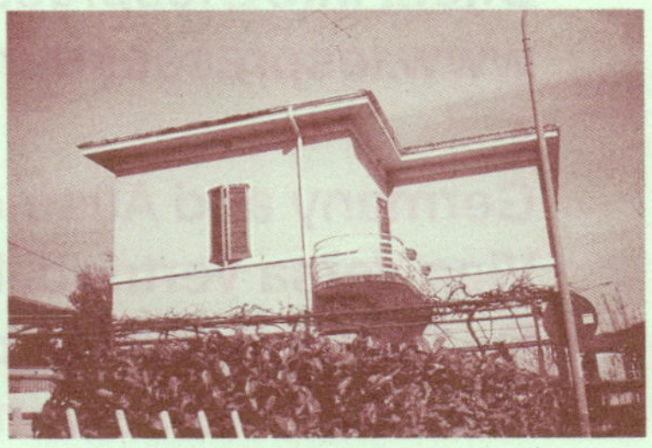
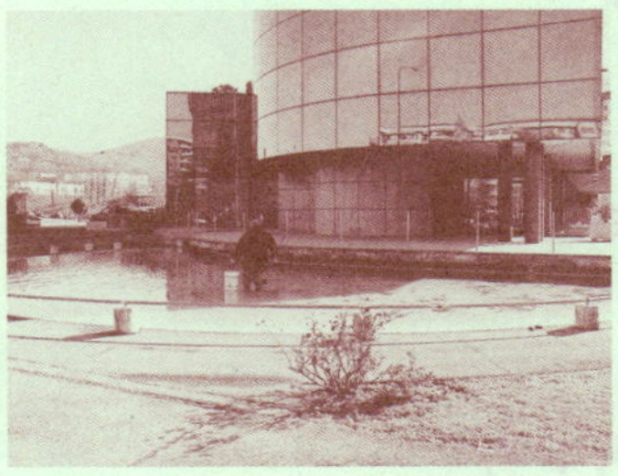
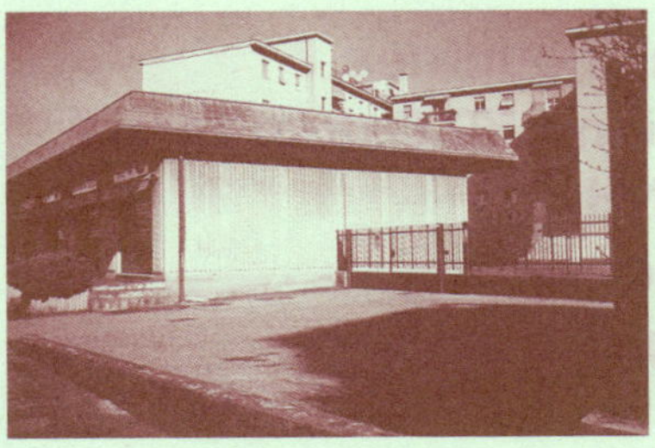
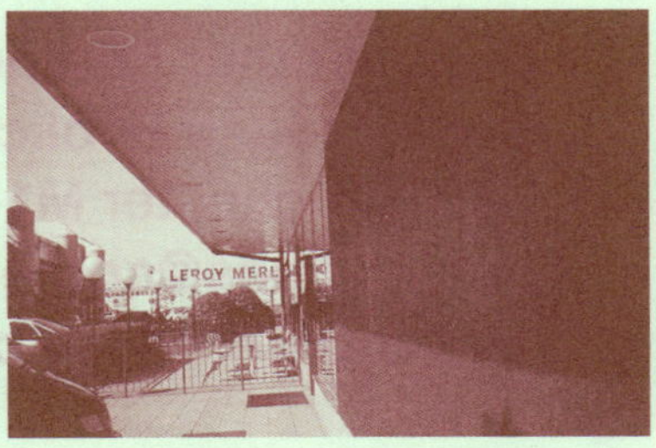
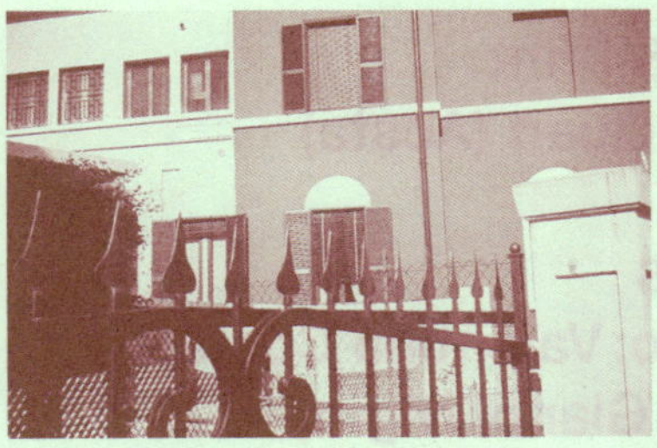
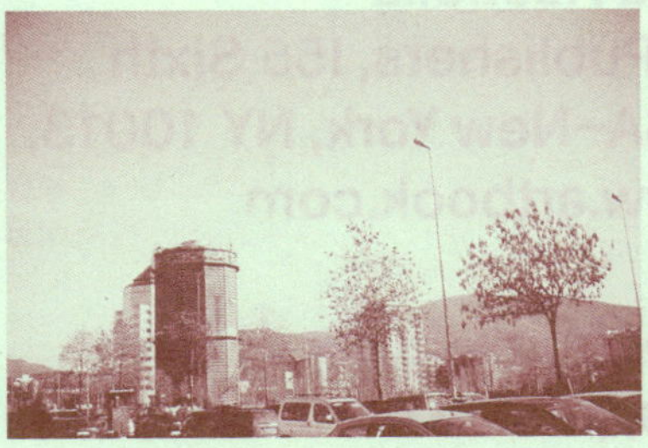
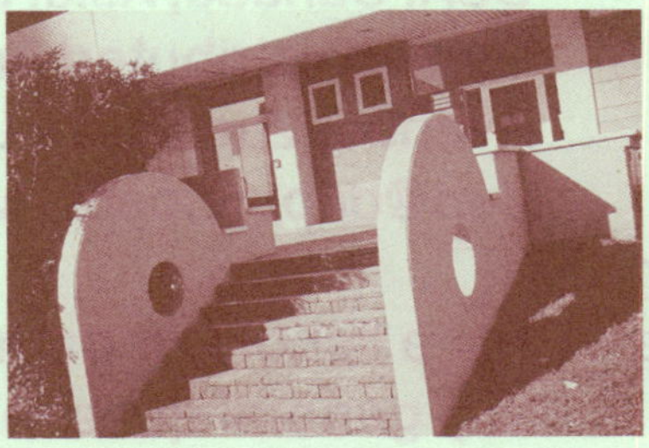
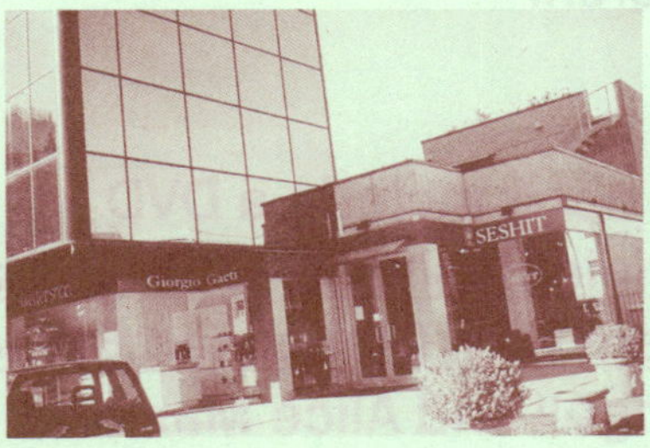
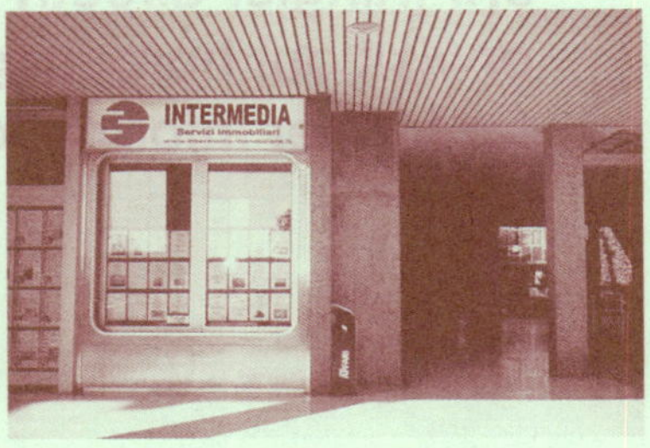

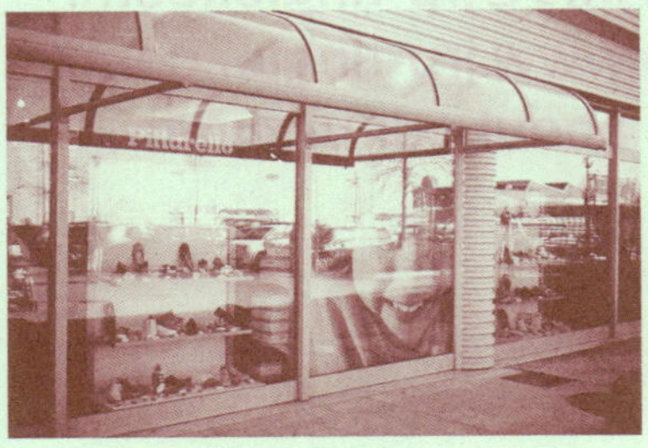
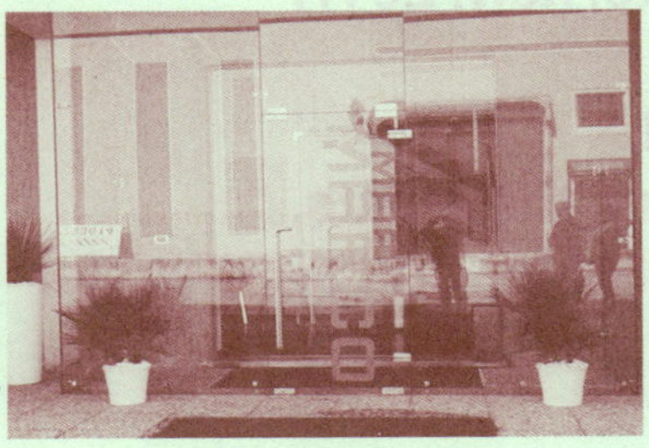
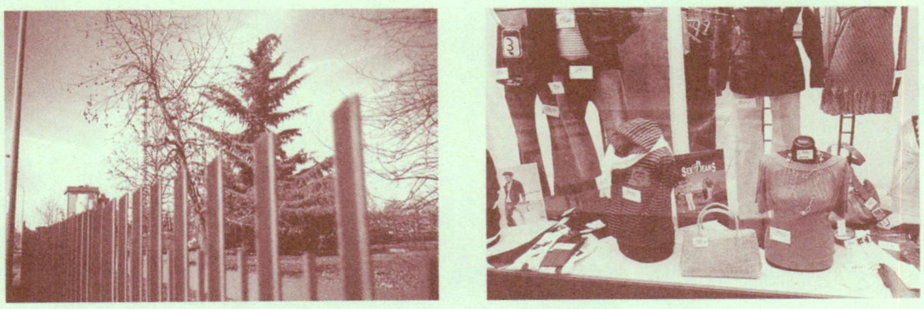

Dan Graham

This book was published on the occasion of the exhibition Dan Graham—Gabriele Basilico. Unidentified Modern City. Globalized Brescia, curated by Maurizio Bortolotti at Galleria Massimo Minini, Brescia, April 2–May 21, 2011.

Edited by
Maurizio Bortolotti, Lionel Bovier & Massimo Minini

Editorial Coordination
Nicola Mafessoni

Editing and Proofreading
Clare Manchester

Texts
Gabriele Basilico, Maurizio Bortolotti, Dan Graham, Massimo Minini

Translations
LogoService, Brescia

Design
Gavillet & Rust / Eigenheer, Geneva

Typeface
Antique (François Rappo)

Color Separation & Print
Musumeci S.p.A., Quart (Aosta)

Acknowledgments
A special thanks to: Valentina Costa, Nicola Mafessoni, Gianni Nigro, and Lorenza Patriarchi

Special edition
200 copies of the book include a DVD of the movie Gabriele Basilico—Dan Graham. Unidentified Modern City. Globalized Brescia by Giampiero D'Angeli and Alice Maxia (Giart–Visioni d'arte, Italy, 2011)

Printed in Europe

Published by
JRP|Ringier
Letzigraben 134
CH–8047 Zurich
T +41 (0) 43 311 27 50
F +41 (0) 43 311 27 51
E info@jrp-ringier.com
www.jrp-ringier.com

ISBN 978-3-03764-218-4

JRP|Ringier books are available internationally at selected bookstores and from the following distribution partners:

Switzerland
Buch 2000, AVA Verlagsauslieferung AG, Centralweg 16, CH–8910 Affoltern a.A., buch2000@ava.ch, www.ava.ch

France
Les presses du réel, 35 rue Colson, F–21000 Dijon, info@lespressesdureel.com, www.lespressesdureel.com

Germany and Austria
Vice Versa Vertrieb, Immanuelkirchstrasse 12, D–10405 Berlin, info@vice-versa-vertrieb.de, www.vice-versa-vertrieb.de

UK and other European countries
Cornerhouse Publications, 70 Oxford Street, UK–Manchester M1 5NH, publications@cornerhouse.org, www.cornerhouse.org/books

USA, Canada, Asia, and Australia
D.A.P./Distributed Art Publishers, 155 Sixth Avenue, 2nd Floor, USA–New York, NY 10013, dap@dapinc.com, www.artbook.com

For a list of our partner bookshops or for any general questions, please contact JRP|Ringier directly at info@jrp-ringier.com, or visit our homepage www.jrp-ringier.com for further information about our program.